Trailblazers

Trailblazers

The Story of Port Arthur Kansallisseura
Loyal Finns in Canada
1926 - 2002

Raili Garth
Kaarina Brooks

Toronto, Ontario, Canada

Copyright © 2010 by
Raili Garth and Kaarina Brooks

All rights reserved.

No part of this book may be
reproduced in any form without
crediting the source.

First published in 2010 by
Jack Lake Productions Inc.
Toronto Ontario Canada

Reprinted in 2018 by
Wisteria Publications
New Tecumseth Ontario Canada

Cover design and layout by
Taria van Weesenbeek

Cover Photograph Credits:

Front: Kansallisseura camp (collection of Pentti Junni)
Back: Kansallisseura members at a picnic in 1927 (Kansallisseura archives)
Skiers at Kansallisseura camp (collection of Pentti Junni)
Nor-Shor Club Dancers at Tapiola in 1970 (collection of Pentti Junni)

ISBN: 978-1-988763-02-6

Dedication

This book is dedicated to all enterprising Finnish immigrants, who began a new life in Canada, and laboured honestly for their families and for society. They adapted to life in their new homeland, and became respected and law-abiding citizens. They were thankful that this new, precious homeland allowed them to love their native country and practice their own culture with no restrictions. Today their descendants have the opportunity to enter various fields of study, and are distinguishing themselves in their life here. To these descendants we want to offer this glimpse into the life of their forebears in words and pictures.

Omistus

Tämä kirja on omistettu kaikille yritteliäille suomalaisille siirtolaisille, jotka aloittivat uuden elämänsä Kanadassa ja tekivät rehellistä työtä oman perheensä ja yhteiskunnan hyväksi. He sopeutuivat uuden kotimaansa elämään ja olivat kunnioitettuja ja lainkuuliaisia tämän maan kansalaisia. He olivat kiitollisia että tämä uusi, kallis kotimaa salli heidän rakastaa omaa isänmaataan ja harrastaa omaa kulttuuriaan ilman esteitä. Tänään heidän jälkeläisensä voivat opiskella eri aloilla, ja ovat monin tavoin edustavia elämässään täällä. Näille jälkeläisille haluamme tarjota tämän katsauksen heidän esi-isiensä elämään sanoin ja kuvin.

Raili Garth
Kaarina Brooks
Pentti Junni

Toronto, Ontario, Canada 2010

Table of Contents

9	**Foreword**
11	**The Beginning**
20	**The Missing Years**
24	**Surprise Lake Camp**
24	Searching for a Home
25	Home at Last!
36	**Celebrations**
36	Kalevala Day
37	Independence Day
42	Anniversaries
49	**Culture**
49	Choirs
51	Discussion and Debating Club
52	Library and Publications
57	**Social Events**
58	*Juhannus* (Midsummer)
61	Social Evenings
66	Theatre
68	*Pikkujoulut* (Christmas Parties)
70	**Charitable Work**
71	Finnish Aid Society
72	Kansallisseura War Effort
79	Fundraising in Later Years

82	**Sports**	
82		Sports and Gymnastic Club Kiri
85		Winter Sports
86		Surprise Lake Swim
92	**Women's Activities**	
96	**Youth Groups**	
96		Finnish Canadian Club (1947 – 1950)
98		Nor-Shor Club (1957 – 1962)
101		Nor-Shor Club Dancers (1964 – 1971)
104	**Noteworthy Members**	
104		Founding Members
104		Honorary Members
107		Kosti Koivukoski
108		Pentti Junni
108		Toini Jacobson
110	**"The Big Picture"**	
110		Kansallisseura and Finland
113		The Central Organization
116	**The End**	
121	Appendix I	Chronology
122	Appendix II	Surprise Lake Swim Results
131	Appendix III	Kansallisseura Members
138	Appendix IV	References

Foreword

When Pentti Junni, the last chairman of Port Arthur Kansallisseura, asked us in the spring of 2008 if we would be interested in writing a history of the now-disbanded club, we eagerly took on the challenge. Kansallisseura had been an important part of our late teens, and the thought of recording the history of its activities throughout the years piqued our interest.

Excited by this idea, we drove to Thunder Bay one stormy day in April, and returned home with several boxes and a musty little suitcase full of documents. These had been faithfully preserved by Mrs. Toini Jacobson, the club's long-time treasurer, and had been passed on to Pentti Junni upon her death.

As we researched further into the past, we came across an "official" reason for this venture. In a letter to Pentti Junni sent in 1976, Dr. Edward W. Laine of the National Ethnic Archives exhorts Kansallisseura to help Canadian society to gain an understanding of and become informed about the valuable contributions made by ethnic minorities in Canada. "To accomplish this, the cultural minorities should preserve and make their historical materials available to researchers so that a more accurate picture of Canadian history may emerge."[1]

From financial journals, minutes of meetings, membership lists, reams of bills and receipts fastened together with rusty straight pins, and miscellaneous letters and frayed documents, a jumble of details of the club's activities emerged for the periods 1926 to 1934, and 1942 to 2002. To fill in the missing years between 1935 and 1941, we consulted microfilms of back copies of *Canadan Uutiset* from 1927 to 1951. To gain a wider background on this period, we read a number of books and articles on Finnish Canadians. We also listened to an undated taped interview with early members Aarne and Vieno Rita, both now deceased. Throughout the writing process we made numerous phone calls to Pentti Junni whenever a question arose.

Then came the task of collecting photographs to illustrate the text. Unfortunately very few pictures of the earlier times exist, and those that were found in the boxes, often had no date or identification of the subjects. Attempts were made to put names to the faces, but we apologize in advance for any mistakes that occurred.

For added authenticity, we included a number of original, albeit grainy documents, many of which are in Finnish. The translations are by the authors, who accept responsibility for any errors. Generous translation assistance was provided by Eine Rossi in Finland.

In the book, the name "Kansallisseura" is reserved for the Port Arthur branch, while the central organization is identified fully as Central Organization of Loyal Finns in Canada (COLFC). Similarly other branches of the society, when mentioned, are called by their full names.

Although the roots of the Kansallisseura movement lie in the politically charged relationship between the Reds and Whites in the early days of Finnish immigration to Canada, this book is not about that. Readers looking for the history of this conflict must go to other sources. Our mandate for this book was to give an overview of the 76-year history of the Port Arthur Kansallisseura. We chose to surround the cold historical facts we found in the records in an aura of warm intimacy. We wanted to bring to life the members who created these records, so the reader could visualize them as people, rather than merely as names on a membership list. We provided glimpses into the day-to-day life of the club—its meetings, the social evenings, its search for a home. The book is thoroughly researched and accurately documented, but we like to think of it as an informal history—a story of people and their activities that reflects the times in which they lived.

There are a number of people to whom we are grateful for their part in this endeavour. First of these is the late Mrs. Toini Jacobson, who had the foresight to preserve every scrap of paper that came to her possession. And since she was such a central member of the club for so many years, the amount of paper was impressive. Next is Pentti Junni, who provided valuable insight into the club's activities during his tenure as chairman.

Special thanks go out to Lakehead University in Thunder Bay and to York University in Toronto for making the microfilm of *Canadan Uutiset* available for consultation. And *kiitos* to Sirpa Kaukinen for reading over an early copy of the manuscript and for giving us her encouraging comments.

A number of people loaned us photographs that have been identified in the text. Our thanks go out to: Pentti Junni, the estate of Erkki Sirén, Väinö Jacobson Jr., Pekka Kuisma, the estate of Toini Parviainen, and especially the estate of Marjatta Ylikorpi. Marjatta's enthusiasm in recording the club's activities with her box camera resulted in an excellent visual record of Kansallisseura events in the late 1950s and early 1960s. In addition to photographs, Mrs. Ellen Koivukoski donated a binder of newspaper clippings from the archives of her father-in-law, Mr. Kosti Koivukoski, delivered to us by Allan Albrecht.

The Port Arthur Kansallisseura *fonds d'archives* will be housed in the archives at Lakehead University in Thunder Bay, Ontario, Canada, where it will be available to anyone wishing to do more research on this interesting topic.

Raili Garth
Kaarina Brooks

Toronto, Ontario, Canada 2010

---

[1] Letter dated February 22, 1976 from Public Archives Canada, Historical Branch, sent by Edward W. Laine, Ph.D., Co-ordinator, Northern European Program, National Ethnic Archives to Mr. Pentti Junni.

The Beginning

The history of *Port Arthurin Kansallisseura* (Finnish National Society) began in Port Arthur in 1926 at a meeting called by Mr. Kosti Koivukoski for Friday, January 22, at the home of Mr. and Mrs. Leonard Mäki. But the roots of the movement are buried in the Finnish Civil War, which raged briefly in 1918, after Finland declared independence from Russia. When the Reds lost, many of them immigrated to the United States and Canada, where they were welcomed by the local branches of *Canadan Suomalainen Järjestö* (CSJ), a leftist organization.[1]

Non-socialist Finns in Port Arthur had already tried in 1917 to establish an association to band together against the socialists. But the new organization, called *Kansallis-Liitto* (Finnish National

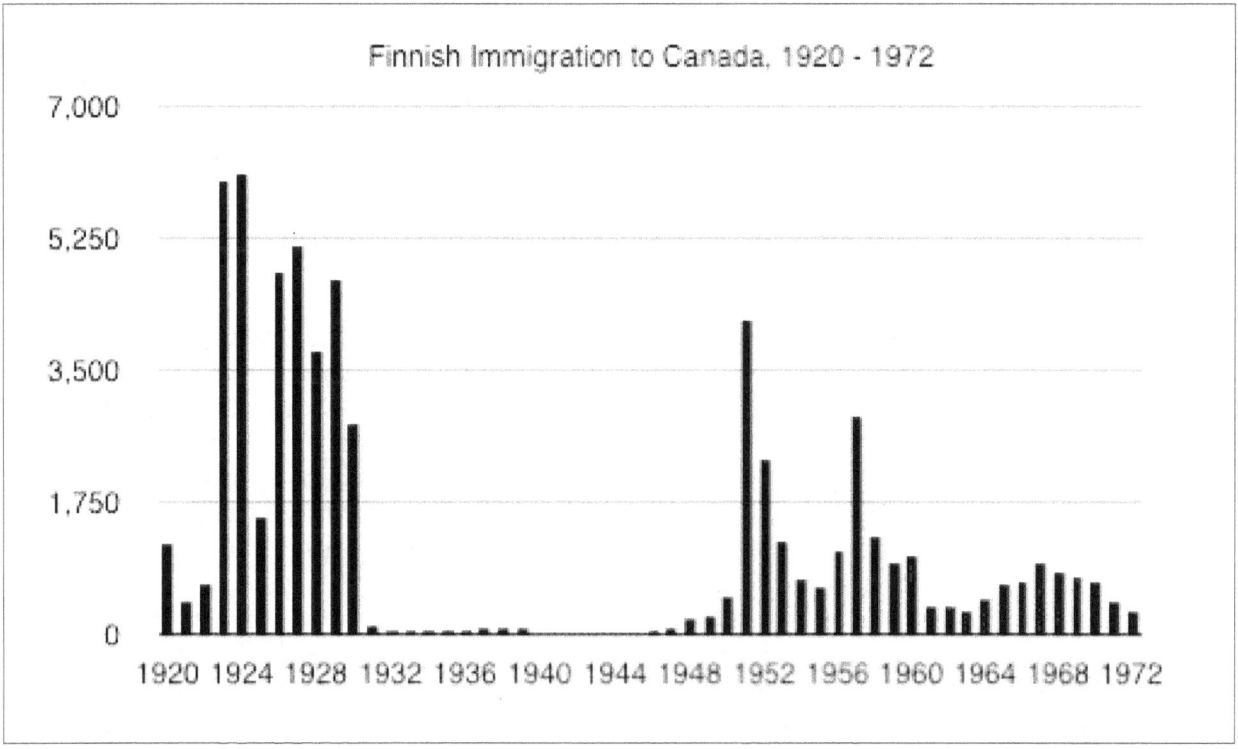

Immigration of Finns to Canada from 1920 to 1972[4]

Federation) did not survive, and soon stopped its operation without establishing a national presence.[2]

"During the 1920's, the pace of Finnish immigration again intensified. This was due in part to the implementation of a quota system for immigration in the United States in 1921 and 1924, which functioned to reduce the Finland-U.S.A. migration flow in favour of Canada. Equally important was the frequent inclusion of Finland as one of the more preferred sources of immigrants by the government of Canada."[3] As a result of this increase in immigration, by 1926 Canada had about 60,000 Finns.

Many of these new immigrants had supported the White side in the Civil War, and problems arose when they collided with the Reds in the various Finnish communities, such as Port Arthur. "CSJ tried to prevent the White Finns from getting work and made use of workplace terrorism, if necessary. New immigrants were called before a special investigation committee and if they could prove that they had belonged to a Red organization, they were given *toveriluotto* (trust of comrades) and *punainen passi* (red passport)."[5] Without this passport, it was difficult to obtain work.

It was thus not surprising that an enthusiastic welcome was given in Port Arthur to the new nationalistic club, Kansallisseura Turisti. For some time its founders had felt the need to bring together like-minded Finns in an organization of their own. A long article in the February 18, 1926 issue of *Canadan Uutiset* echoed this sentiment:

"Above all, this newly established club tries to awaken and maintain in Finns a national feeling in all its aspects. In addition, it impresses upon the members to honour the laws of this land and keep peace in the community. In general the activity of the club will be conducted in a spirit that is true to both Finland and Canada. This concept leads to personal freedom, equality and harmony in all things.

"We wish Kansallisseura Turisti much luck and success as it begins to perform its far-reaching work in the field of Finnish nationalism. We are sure that from this tiny seed will eventually grow a great tree that, with time, will spread its roots into all Finnish-Canadian communities, and will gather our immigrant nation into a unified entity."

The event was even noticed in the United States and reported in the March 3 issue of *New Yorkin Uutiset* after Kansallisseura had held its first social event.

"This new club has put on its first social evening this month on the 17th, and based on the program, it was very successful. All nationalistic Finns in Port Arthur attended and enthusiasm was high. This shows that the White Finnish population in Canada is awakening to action in the same way as here in the United States and, of course, nationalists in other Canadian communities will follow the example set by Port Arthur Finns, and establish social and cultural clubs at locations that have an adequate number of our countrymen.

"Experience has shown that participating in church activities alone is not enough even among Canadian Finns, and that other nationalistic activity is required to raise the cultural level, and strengthen the feeling of togetherness."

Thus fortified with good wishes, the new Kansallisseura Turisti set out to do its patriotic work throughout the Finnish community in Port Arthur. Such a large task for such a young club! But it was fortunate to have "...powerful support from the Finnish consuls who legitimized its goals and gave the government of Finland's official approval to its work. The first Consul General of Finland, Akseli Rauanheimo (1923-1932) hoped the organization would improve the reputation of Finns in Canada."[6]

PÖYTÄKIRJA,

tehty Kansallisseuran perustavassa kokouksessa Port Arthurissa, Ont., Canada, joka kokous pidettiin Mr. ja Mrs. Leonard Mäen asunnolla, 324 Pearl St., tammikuun 22 p:nä 1926, alkaen kello 8 illalla.

1.

Kokous valitsi yksimielisesti Mr. Kosti Koivukosken puheenjohtajaksi. Kirjuriksi valittiin Mrs. Hilja Korte.

2.

Puheenjohtaja esitti kysymyksen, pidetäänkö tämä kokous Kansallisseuran perustavana kokouksena. Joku läsnäolijoista esitti, että se sellaisena pidettäisiin. Esitystä kannatettiin ja päätökseksi tuli, että tämä kokous on Kansallisseuran perustava kokous. Niinollen oli seura perustettu.

3.

Esitettiin kysymys, onko tällä kokouksella valta päättää seuran säännöistä. Yksimielinen päätös oli myönteinen.

4.

Tuotiin esille, että väliaikainen toimikunta on laatinut sääntöehdotuksen perus- ja ohjesääntöjä varten.

5.

Sääntökomitealla oli seuralle seuraavat nimiehdotukset: Kansallisseura "Turisti", Kansallisseura "Saimaa" ja Kansallisseura "Pohjola". Uusia nimiehdotuksia ei ilmaantunut, joten kolmesta tarjolla olleesta hyväksyttiin yksimielisesti seuran nimeksi Kansallisseura "Turisti". Seuran kotipaikka on Port Arthur, Ont., Canada.

6.

Puheenjohtaja luki sääntöehdotuksen pykälä pykälältä perussääntöjen 10:nteen pykälään asti, jotka kaikki kokous hyväksyi pienillä muutoksilla.

Minutes of the founding meeting of Kansallisseura Turisti, January 22, 1926

The following is a translation of the minutes of the founding meeting, shown on the previous page:

"Minutes
recorded at the founding meeting of Kansallisseura in Port Arthur, Ont., Canada, which was held at the home of Mr. and Mrs. Leonard Mäki, 324 Pearl St., on January 22, 1926, beginning at 8 p.m.

#1.
Mr. Kosti Koivukoski was unanimously chosen as chairman. Mrs. Hilja Korte was chosen as secretary.

#2.
The chairman asked whether this should be considered the founding meeting of Kansallisseura. One of the members moved that it should be thus. The motion carried and it was decided that this meeting should be the founding meeting of Kansallisseura. So the club was formed.

#3.
Question was raised whether this meeting had the authority to decide on the rules for the club. The favourable vote was unanimous.

#4.
The members were advised that a temporary committee has drawn up a list of tentative rules of procedure for the club.

#5.
The Rules Committee proposed the following names for the club: Kansallisseura 'Turisti', Kansallisseura 'Saimaa' and Kansallisseura 'Pohjola'. There were no new suggestions for names, so from the three possibilities Kansallisseura 'Turisti' was unanimously chosen as the name for the club. The location of the club is Port Arthur, Ont., Canada.

#6.
The chairman read the first ten tentative rules of procedure, which were all passed with slight modifications."

According to Ahti Tolvanen[7], the constitution of the new society was based on the nationalist Youth Organization, *Suomen Nuorisoseura*. The rules below are not the ones discussed at the founding meeting, but were handed to Kansallisseura by the Central Organization of Loyal Finns in Canada (COLFC) in 1933, when the Port Arthur branch joined it.

First three rules for Port Arthur Kansallisseura

The rules state in part:

1. "Name and location of the club.
2. The purpose of the organization is to unite the Finnish people of the community and the surrounding area in a patriotic and enlightening manner and, as a club, raise their spiritual and material level, keep a connection to the old homeland, make Finland and Finns known to Canadians, and Canada and Canadians known to Finns, thus producing respectable citizens for Canada.
3. To this end the club shall:
a) organize patriotic festivities,
b) hold social evenings with performances to support the club's activities,
c) establish within the club theatre, music, sport, discussion etc. groups, and

in this manner give the members an opportunity to develop both their physical and spiritual abilities,
d) help members in extreme financial distress, if the resources of the club are sufficient and if the executive deems it justifiable,
e) help Finland."

On Sunday, January 24, the executive committee held its first meeting, electing the following slate of officers, who have also been identified in Appendix III- "Kansallisseura Members":

Chairman	Mr. Kosti Koivukoski
Vice-Chairman	Mr. Leonard W. Mäki
Secretary	Mrs. Hilja Korte
Memb. Secretary	Miss Maiju Lehtonen
Treasurer	Mr. Lauri Maunu
Bookkeeper	Mr. Niilo Kyrö
General Manager	Mr. Erick J. Korte
Deputy Members	Mrs. Vieno Paananen
	Mr. Kalle Virtanen
	Mr. Väinö Pentti
Auditors	Mr. H. W. Niinimäki
	Mr. R. Schrey

From the records of the first few meetings, it appears that there were approximately 34 founding members. Twenty-nine of them have been identified in Appendix III. Membership grew quickly and by the end of the first year, the club had about 134 members.

New members filled in an application form that had to be approved by the executive. (This rule was discontinued sometime in the 1960s.) Initially new members had to pay an application fee, but this was abolished in a meeting on April 17, 1928. At this same meeting the name of the club was changed to *Port Arthurin Kansallisseura* (Finnish National Society) with the dropping of the word Turisti. The Finnish version of the name remained essentially constant, except for occasional reference in the later years to *Port Arthurin Suomalainen Kansallisseura*. After Port Arthur joined COLFC, it was also called Loyal Finns in Canada, Port Arthur Branch.

At this same meeting the membership fee was decreased to $1.00. It was not until 1976 that the fee was increased to $2.00 and then, in 1981 to $3.00, to $5.00 in 1985, and finally to $10.00 in 1998.

The first event held by the new club was the Kalevala celebration on Sunday, February 28, just over a month after the founding meeting. According to an undated article in *Canadan Uutiset* describing the event, Sons of England Hall was almost full of "nationalistic" audience members. The "thoughtfully selected" program, performed to "a high standard",

Membership card for Port Arthur Kansallisseura

Ad for the opening ceremony of the newly formed Kansallisseura Turisti in Canadan Uutiset, *March 4, 1926*

was well received, and so, right from the start, Kansallisseura began to fulfill one of its objectives—organize patriotic festivities.

The official *alkajaisjuhla* (opening ceremony), held on March 10, was promoted extensively in *Canadan Uutiset*, and reported at length in the March 18 issue:

"The opening ceremonies for Kansallisseura Turisti, held on Wednesday of the past week at Sons of England Hall, fulfilled all the hopes and anticipations that could reasonably be raised for this first social evening of Kansallisseura. Above all, the whole event had a homey and comfortable feeling that became more and more evident as the evening wore on. Audience filled the large hall."

Missing from the list of performances in the ad are a solo by Mrs. W. Jacobson, piano solos by Miss Kathleen Paananen and Miss Helmi Lassi, recital by Miss Hulda Rinne, songs by the new mixed Kansallisseura choir conducted by Mr. Kosti Koivukoski, and a keynote address by Mr. Leonard Mäki. "*Kaiken kukkana oli Mr. Koivukosken hauskat savolaiset kubletit, jotka yleisö otti vastaan niin suurella riemastuksella, että se ajoittain tahtoi tehdä haittaa laulajan esitykselle.*"[8] (The crowning touch was comic songs in Savo dialect by Mr. Koivukoski, which the audience received with such rejoicing that at times the laughter tended to interfere with the performance.) The evening resulted in a profit of $65.00 and much goodwill towards the new club.

And so Kansallisseura was launched, and during its first year it held many other events such as a family night, a Flower dance, Midsummer celebrations in Nolalu, and an outdoor event at Nikander's farm.

There was another outdoor event on Labour Day, a young men's dance in October, Independence Day celebrations, and a Christmas party at Wallace Hall.

Before the first annual meeting, a *kruunauskomitea* (Crowning Committee)

Mr. Paananen, Mr. K. Justin, Mr. Matti Puustinen, Mr. Ralph Poutanen, Mr. Niilo Kyrö and other unidentified members of Kansallisseura at a picnic in 1927 (Photo from Kansallisseura archives)

Jäsenhakemus N:o

PORT ARTHUR :n Kansallisseuran Johtokunnalle.

Anon täten päästä jäseneksi **Kanadan Kansallismielisten Suomalaisten Liiton** paikalliseen jäsenseuraan, jossa tarkoituksessa annan alempana olevat, täten oikeiksi vakuuttamani henkilötiedot itsestäni. Jos tämä hakemukseni hyväksytään,

1 Lupaan noudattaa ja kunniassa pitää tämän maan lakeja sekä K. K. S. liiton ja sen paikallisen jäsenseuran periaatteita ja sääntöjä;

2 Tahdon esiintymisessäni ja toiminnassani niin hyvin seurassa kuin sen ulkopuolellakin koettaa olla kunniaksi sekä K. K. S. Liitolle että koko suomalaiselle kansallisuudelle;

3 Lupaan voimieni ja kykyjeni mukaan toimia ja työskennellä K. K. S. Liiton sekä sen paikallisen jäsenseuran hyväksi.

4 Vakuutan, että en hyväksy enkä kannata kommunismia tahi muita suuntia ja virtauksia, jotka sotivat lainalaista yhteiskuntamuotoa, maan lakeja tahi hyviä tapoja vastaan.

PORT ARTHUR :ssa, MARRAS kuun 28 p. 1959

Nimi: Raimo Mäntysalo

Täysi nimi Suomessa ja täällä: RAIMO MÄNTYSALO
Osoite ja puhelin: 216 McINTYRE ST. 41683
Syntymäpaikka ja -aika: VIIPURI 18.12.1935
Kotipaikka Suomessa: HELSINKI
Naimisissa tai naimaton: NAIMATON
Kanadaan tuloaika: 18.9.1959
Minkä maan kansalainen: SUOMEN

Kuulunut tai kuuluu seuraaviin yhdistyksiin ja seuroihin (aika ja erikoistehtävät mainittavat):

Suomessa:

Kanadassa:

Suosittelemme yllä olevaa hakemusta hyväksyttäväksi:

Nimi: .... Nimi: ....
(Suosittelijoiden on oltava Kansallisseuran jäseniä)

Hyväksytty: .... Jäsenkirjan numero: ....

Eronnut, eroitettu, siirtynyt: ....

Eroamisen, eroittamisen syy: ....
(Tarpeettomat sanat pyyhitään yli)

Puheenjohtaja: Toivo Sikkilä

Jäsenkirjuri: ....

Membership application for Raimo Mäntysalo from 1959

was set up. Its purpose was to ensure that the installation of the next chairman would be done with "due dignity". Because of time restrictions the ceremony was never actualized, but the suggestion can be interpreted as an attempt to elevate the tone of the new organization. At the end of the first year the financial committee reported an income of $415.66, expenses of $382.26, leaving $33.40 in the bank account. The club also owned $150.00 worth of restaurant equipment.

And so Port Arthur Kansallisseura ended its first successful year, ready to take on the next seventy-five.

---

[1] Raivio, Yrjö, *Kanadan Suomalaisten Historia*, (Vancouver: New West Press Co. Ltd., 1975) p. 464.
[2] Toiviainen, Lauri, *75-vuotias Vapaa Sana*, (Toronto: Vapaa Sana Press Ltd., 2008) p. 110.
[3] Saarinen, Oiva, "Geographical Perspectives on Finnish Canadian Immigration and Settlement," *Polyphony: The Bulletin of the Multicultural History Society of Ontario, Finns in Ontario,* (Vol. 3, No. 2, Fall 1981) p. 18-20.
[4] Ibid., p. 17.
[5] Raivio, Y., *Kanadan Suomalaisten Historia*, op. cit. p. 464.
[6] Lindström Varpu et al, "The Finnish Canadian Communities during the decade of Depression," *Karelian Exodus: Journal of Finnish Studies,* (Vol. 8, No. 1, August, 2004) p. 24.
[7] Tolvanen, Ahti, *Finntown, A Perspective on Urban Integration, Port Arthur Finns in the Inter-war Period: 1918 – 1939*, (University of Helsinki, Finn Forum, 1984) p. 68.
[8] *Canadan Uutiset*, March 18, 1926.

The Missing Years

There is a curious gap of nine years in the existing records of Port Arthur Kansallisseura between 1933 and 1941. No minutes of meetings for the club exist for the years from 1933 to 1948. Financial journals did not appear until 1942. The only other documentation found in Kansallisseura files for this period is *Siirtolainen,* a publication for Christmas, 1933. The general feeling is that records for the missing years have been lost or destroyed, but the authors believe that another explanation is also possible.

The authors suggest that Kansallisseura may have been somewhat "dormant" for some of these years, with members initially directing their activities to churches, and then later to the charitable activities associated with the war in Finland. Since no club records exist, the only proof for this can be found in the annals of *Canadan Uutiset*, which faithfully published the activities of the Finnish community in Port Arthur at that time.

First indications that interest in Kansallisseura was diminishing in the early 1930s were found in articles, such as the one on February 21, 1934, which states that the past year had been difficult for the club, but women were becoming more active, and it was hoped that men would follow. A letter to the editor in the November 28 issue of the same year complained that Kansallisseura was not active enough in helping people, allowing the Left to become more prominent.

Another indication of waning activity was the fact that the Independence Day celebrations in 1934 were held in conjunction with the church. The program was similar to previous years, and the collection of $20.90 was sent to Homes for the Homeless Children, the traditional beneficiary of this event. However, although Mr. Kosti Koivukoski spoke as usual, there was no mention of Kansallisseura in the newspaper article. The following year Kansallisseura was not involved at all in the Independence Day celebrations, which were again held in the church.

The few Kansallisseura activities reported by *Canadan Uutiset* during the end of 1934 and the beginning of 1935 were those put on by *Käsityökerho* (Needlecraft Club). It appears that the men had not taken up the challenge to become involved, as mentioned earlier, perhaps because they were away looking for work during the Depression.

It is possible that for some reason *Canadan Uutiset* was not reporting the activities of Port Arthur Kansallisseura. Someone in the "north" wrote a letter to the editor in the September 5, 1934 issue, wondering why *Canadan Uutiset* published so few articles about the club's activities. Another letter in the April 11, 1935 issue complained that Kansallisseura had, in fact, been active, but this had not been reported. The club was said to be holding weekly dances, and Sointu choir was awake again, and holding practices. This was confirmed by an undated article from an English newspaper, probably from 1935, found in the files of Kosti Koivukoski, which stated "The Finnish National Society in Port Arthur, now considered a branch of the Central Organization of Loyal Finns in Canada, meets once a month for business and twice a month for socials and entertainments."

On January 13, 1935 the annual meeting of Kansallisseura was held at the home of Mrs. Ida Virtanen. One of the members brought up the usual question: When is Kansallisseura going to build on the lot that it owns? However, since the *Evankelis-luterilainen Kansalliskirkko* (Finnish Lutheran Church) had completed a new church building in 1934 at 262 Wilson Street, it was felt there was no money in the community to proceed with another communal building. According to the article in the January 16 issue of *Canadan Uutiset*, the discussion became rather heated, until it was cut off by the speaker's wife, "*Joten kokous päättyi rauhallisesti eikä niin ollen Kansallisseuran rauhaa päässyt häiritsemään paremmin kansallinen kuin isänmaallinenkaan innostus.*" (So the meeting ended peacefully, and thus the peace of Kansallisseura was not disturbed by either national or patriotic enthusiasm.) Ouch! This was the last Kansallisseura annual meeting written up in *Canadan Uutiset* until 1942.

The last social event reported for Kansallisseura for this period was the Kalevala Centennial in February, 1935 that attracted 175 people, who enjoyed an uplifting program. The last Kansallisseura monthly meeting recorded in the pages of *Canadan Uutiset* for several years was in March at the home of Mrs. Ida Virtanen. If, in fact, Kansallisseura was still operating after this date, its activities were not reported by the newspaper, nor recorded in any minutes or financial journals.

It appears that all the branches of the Central Organization of Loyal Finns in Canada (COLFC) had been feeling lethargic, because at the COLFC annual meeting on March 10, 1935 in Port Arthur it was reported "*Liiton toiminta on nyt entisestään vakiintunut.*" (The activity of the league is now more regular than in the past.) Two new chapters had been established and all branches were encouraged to start collecting funds to send the Finnish Olympic team to Berlin in 1936. A total of almost $500.00 was eventually sent to Finland, but there is no record of any contribution by the Port Arthur branch. In April of 1935 COLFC also suggested that member clubs help plan religious services – something that was not completely supported by the letters to the editor that followed.

But it appears that Kansallisseura members in Port Arthur were becoming more involved in the church. The March 26, 1936 issue of *Canadan Uutiset* reported that religious activity had been strong lately. This was supported by Ahti Tolvanen's findings that "in the latter thirties the Lutheran church seems to have experienced a spurt of activity when prominent individuals in the community like...the National Society's secretary, Mrs. V. Latvala, took leadership positions in the Congregation."[1] A reading of the section on "*Kirkollista Toimintaa*" ("Ecclesiastical Activities") in *Canadan Uutiset* confirmed that the names of many leading Kansallisseura members appeared there regularly. For example, the *Käsityökerho*, led by Mrs. Irene Suline, met as usual, except that a prayer by the pastor had been added to the start of the meetings, which were now held in the church, instead of members' homes. Mr. Kosti Koivukoski led the church choir. Also, the only reported social events in Port Arthur —except for those held at the leftist *Työn Temppeli* (Labour Temple)—were put on by the church. The programs were very similar to the *Iltamat* (Social Evenings) held in the past by Kansallisseura, but the dance at the end had been replaced by cups of coffee. The program listings showed that the same people who had performed at the *Iltamat*, now exhibited their talents in the church, rather than at Sons of England Hall. In fact few, if any ads for dances in Port Arthur appeared in the pages of *Canadan Uutiset* until May of 1938.

For the rest of 1936, 1937, and 1938 the names of many Kansallisseura members continued to appear regularly under "Ecclesiastical Activities". The Easter Sunday choral evening, reported in the March 31, 1937 issue of *Canadan Uutiset*, was a good example of the change that had taken place in the social life of Port Arthur. The list of performers resembled the Kansallisseura social evenings of the past: piano solo by Mr. Armas Laakso, two solos by Mrs. Vera Jacobson, piano solo by Miss Helmi Anderson, solo by Miss Lilian Mäki accompanied by Miss Aini Rantanen, poem by Mrs. Rauha Niinimäki, solo by Mr. Kosti Koivukoski, and many religious songs sung by the 30-member mixed choir. It was praised as "...*tekevät siunattua työtä seurakunnan hyväksi*" (...doing blessed work for the good of the congregation).

This situation continued until the start of the Finnish Winter War on November 29, 1939. *Suomen Avustusyhdistys* (Finnish Aid Society) was established and people belonging to all the Finnish clubs in Port Arthur, except those on the Left, now directed their combined efforts to help raise funds for the Finnish war effort. Since many Kansallisseura members seemed to be wholly involved in its activities until 1942, the authors feel that a partial history of this organization belongs in this book. See "Finnish Aid Society" on page 71 for more details.

The first stirrings of the re-awakening of Port Arthur Kansallisseura were found in a short notice in the May 14, 1941 issue of *Canadan Uutiset.*

Notice of meeting to re-start Kansallisseura in 1941

"Summons to a meeting.

The members of Port Arthur Kansallisseura and former members of Sointu-choir are requested to attend a meeting at *Suomi Tupa* on Friday, the 16th of this month at 8 p.m. Important issue to be discussed.

K. Koivukoski, Honorary Chairman."

It was not reported what happened at the meeting, nor what this important issue was, but obviously the club had re-emerged, as shown by the article which appeared in *Canadan Uutiset* on March 11, 1942.

"Kansallisseura Social Evening.

A group of former members of the local Kansallisseura are holding a social evening next Wednesday, March 18 at 8:30 p.m. at the S.O.E. Hall in Port Arthur. (We refer to an ad on another page.)

The purpose of the social evening is to bring again to life our Kansallisseura, which has been 'sleeping' for some time.

We will attempt to compile a complete program for the evening and hope that all loyal true Finns will arrive in great numbers. In these difficult times it is refreshing to get together to have some fun, especially when it happens in the context of true Finnish spirit. Thus let us remember next Wednesday evening—when we will meet!"

Kansallisseuran iltamat

Joukko paikallisen Kansallisseuran entisiä jäseniä toimeenpanee iltamat ensi keskiviikkona t.k. 18 p:nä klo 8.30 illalla, S.O.E. haalilla, Port Arthurissa. (Viittaamme toisessa paikassa olevaan ilmoitukseen.)

Iltaman tarkoituksena on uudelleen henkiin virvoittaa Kansallisseuramme, joka on ollut "nukuksissa" jo jonkun aikaa. Iltamaan koetetaan varata täysipainoinen ohjelma ja toivotaan, että kaikki kansallismieliset, kunnon suomalaiset saapuvat jonkolla iltamiin. — Näinä vaikeina aikoina on virkistävää kokoontua yhteen saamaan hiukan huviakin, varsinkin kun se tapahtuu kunnon suomalaisuuden merkeissä. — Muistakaamme siis ensi keskiviikkoiltaa — silloin tavataan!

Notice of first social evening to be held by the re-awakened Kansallisseura on March 18, 1942

Starting in 1942, the club's financial journals indicate furious fundraising activity, which culminated in 1946 in the sending of $500.00 to the Canada-Finland Aid Society Fund in Toronto. This is reported in more detail in "Kansallisseura War Effort" on page 72.

Based on the foregoing, the authors suggest that during the years from 1935 to 1939, many Kansallisseura members directed their activities towards the church, and the club itself was mainly dormant. Then, starting in 1939 until the end of 1941, Kansallisseura members, along with other Finnish groups in Port Arthur, were involved with the Finnish Aid Society. These activities could explain the curious gap in the records of Port Arthur Kansallisseura.

---

[1] Tolvanen, Ahti, *Finntown, A Perspective on Urban Integration, Port Arthur Finns in the Inter-war Period: 1918 – 1939,* (University of Helsinki, Finn Forum, 1984) page 17 (footnote).

Surprise Lake Camp

It took almost thirty years and several attempts that went astray, before Kansallisseura finally found its home, with the purchase of an old log cabin at Surprise Lake in 1954.

Searching for a Home

The minutes of February 21, 1926 show that already at this first monthly meeting of the newly-formed Kansallisseura Turisti, Mrs. Tyyne Mäki brought up the idea of finding *"oma huoneisto"*, or a permanent home for the club. The idea of a restaurant was also discussed, for the members felt that *"...ruokailuhomma olisi kovin tarpeeseen"* (...some way of providing food was badly needed.) The restaurant proposal was probably aimed at the numerous single young men who had recently arrived from Finland, reflecting one of the aims of Kansallisseura—helping new immigrants.

The February 25, 1926 issue of *Canadan Uutiset* reported that at this meeting *"...otettiin esille myös kysymys oman ravintolan ja sen yhteyteen mahdollisesti tulevan asuntotalon hommaamisesta seuralle. Lukuisista esilletuoduista mielipiteistä ilmeni, että tällainen 'poikatalo' olisi paikkakunnalla tarpeen vaatima."* (...the question of procuring a restaurant in conjunction with a rooming house to be run by the club was brought up. From the many opinions expressed it became apparent that such a rooming house was considered a necessity for the community.)

The subsequently-formed committee suggested that $5.00 loan/gift certificates should be issued for the total sum of $300.00 to further this idea. Later this committee reported that they were continuing to collect donations and had already purchased $150.00 worth of equipment for the restaurant, but were having considerable trouble finding a suitable location for the building. Eventually, in a meeting on July 7 this ambitious restaurant/rooming house undertaking was abandoned and all the collected monies were returned, except for donations.

In a September, 1926 meeting, the search now re-focused on finding a suitable meeting room for the club. Discussion centered on an apartment in a building owned by Mr. Palomäki that could be rented for $75.00/month. This was considered quite reasonable, but the idea never came to fruition.

Eventually this search for a meeting room was abandoned, and by the beginning of 1929 the club again set its sights on a more ambitious goal—owning its own building. A trial subscription at the beginning of February indicated that the membership was enthusiastically behind this idea. *Canadan Uutiset* wrote about the ensuing spirited meeting: [1]

> Haalihomma edistyy myrskyaskelin, sekä rahaa että innostusta näyttää löytyvän vallan ilahduttavan runsaasti niin vanhemmissa kuin nuoremmissakin jäsenissä ja asiankannattajissa. Ja hätäkö on rahaa löytää, kun kysymyksessä ei olekaan mikään lahjoittaminen tai avustaminen, vaan rahain sijoittaminen tuottavaan liikeyritykseen! — Ei tässä kauvan "nokka tuhise" ennenkuin kutsu kierii ympäri kylää: tulkaa Kansallisseuran oman talon avajais- ja vihkiäisjuhlaan!

Canadan Uutiset *article about a meeting held on February 17, 1929, discussing a building for Kansallisseura*

"The search for a hall is advancing like a storm; both money and enthusiasm can be found in heart-warming quantities in both young and old members and supporters. And why should there be a problem finding funds, when it's not a question of a gift or of charity, but an investment in a profitable enterprise! With this whirlwind of activity it shouldn't take long before an invitation is circulating through the town: 'Come to celebrate the opening and dedication of Kansallisseura's own home!'"

The Independent Labour Party building now became the new target and at the February 24, 1929 meeting it was decided that the purchase should proceed. Mr. Häyrynen was authorized to collect money from men working at bush camps around Port Arthur, and Mr. Koivukoski was asked to contact Mr. Belli regarding the price. But although the fundraising was proceeding well, the club abandoned the idea of buying a home, and instead re-directed its efforts to building one. It was felt that a more spacious facility, better meeting the club's various needs, was required.

Thus, in 1930 Kansallisseura purchased two lots with a 66 foot frontage from the old Temperance Society for $900.00. However, because of the Depression, the club was unable to come up with the necessary building funds. The issue came to a head at the 1935 annual meeting, when a member complained that the club was paying high taxes for the lots and should now build on them. But since the Finns in Port Arthur had completed a new church building in 1934, there was no extra money to go around, and eventually both lots were sold.

In 1950 the club purchased yet another lot on Algoma Street. Mr. Leo Harm offered free architectural drawings for the new building and Mr. Lahti said he would dig the basement for free. But the high taxes again made it a burden, and a year later the lot was sold for the purchase price. Kansallisseura paid back the monies owed to all members who had helped out with expenses.

Then at the June 13, 1954 meeting, Mr. Väinö Jacobson reported that three lots, with 300 feet of shoreline and an old log cabin "that could be fixed up", were for sale next to the Jacobson's cottage at Surprise Lake. Kansallisseura had finally found a home!

Home at Last!

Kansallisseura's 28-year dream of having a home culminated with the purchase of this property. The place was considered ideal, because it would permit the holding of outdoor celebrations and sporting events.

The purchase of the land was handled by Lawyer Kajander. The club paid $60.00 as their share of a ½ mile road to the camp, along with other cottagers. Toini Jacobson was authorized to buy an

19 Päivä Syyskuuta 1954,
         Suririce järvi.

Kansallis seuran kokous pidettiin
Omassa. Rakennuksessa.
Tämä oli ensimmäinen kokous. oman
Katon alla. Lassä oli 15 jäsentä
ja oli työtä ja tauhua. ja pidettiin
Syyskäinen Kokous.

1) Puheen johtaja Väinö Jackson.
avasi Kokouksen. ja toi esille ilonsa
että meillä on alku josta on hyvä
jatkaa. toiseksi hän toi ilmi että
palo vaakutus on otettu. 6,000 tallaria,
Kokous katsoi olevan tämän hyvän.

2) ja Päätettiin panna iltamat
Pystyyn. Ehtätettiin Orensi Haalia.
ja katsottiin olevan kyllin isa
Orensi Haali.
ja valittiin 4 Henkinen Komitea
järjestämään tämän.
    Wera Jackson mrs Sulene
   Mrs niemelä, Mrs Rita
Perjantai iltana ehtätettiin, tähän
tappui Kokous. ja työtauhu jatkui Ellen

Page from Kansallisseura Pöytäkirja *(Minutes), recording the first meeting held at Surprise Lake on September 19, 1954*

A summer day at the old Surprise Lake camp in August of 1959. Can you spot Toivo Erkkilä, Seppo and Veijo Parviainen, Brenda Buick, Reetta and Eija Junni, and Laila and Väinö Mäkelä? (From the collection of Pentti Junni)

old stove for $3.00 to make coffee for the workmen. From an old post office "*rantaasi*" (franchise) that was being torn down, Väinö Jacobson and Jussi Niemelä bought old doors and some windows for the cabin.

It was also decided that everyone who was not a member of Kansallisseura, but who assisted with the work at the camp, would be given a free membership for a year. Some of them, such as Arvo Pärssinen, remained members for years. These free memberships are identified in "Kansallisseura Members" in Appendix III.

Below is a record of the first meeting held at the Surprise Lake camp:

"19 day, September, 1954 Suririce Lake

Kansallisseura meeting was held in our own building. This was the first meeting under our own roof. Present were 15 members, and there was work and activity and we held a short meeting.
1. Chairman Wäinö Jacobson opened the meeting and expressed his joy that we have a beginning from which it is good to continue. Secondly he stated that a fire insurance policy has been purchased. The meeting considered this to be satisfactory.
2. and it was decided to hold a dance. Orange Hall was suggested and it was considered to be large enough. Orensi Haali. And a 4-person committee was chosen to organize this: Wera Jacobson, Mrs. Sulene, Mr. Niemelä, Mr. Rita. Friday night was suggested. This ended the meeting and the work continues. Ellen."

The price of the purchase of Parcel No.10354, Thunder Bay Freehold, on January 24, 1955, was recorded in the club's financial journals as $371.25.

Väinö Jacobson, Irene Suline and Niilo Viitala were registered as trustees for this piece of real estate. Several names for

Receipt from McComber & McComber, lawyers handling the purchase of Surprise Lake camp, dated January 24, 1955

the summer camp were suggested, such as Kesäranta, Tapiola and Koivuranta, but nothing was ever decided. So until it was sold almost 50 years later, the place was always known as *Kansallisseuran kämppä*.

A March, 1955 clipping from *Canadan Uutiset* notified its readers that a summer camp had been purchased by Kansallisseura, but that there was no sauna. To raise money for building one, the ladies held a turkey dinner at Orange Hall on March 20, making a profit of $100.30. A sauna was indeed built in June of that year. It was 12 feet by 16 feet, and the construction material for it cost $265.90, with paint adding another $11.65 to the expenses.

Workers having a break in front of the old camp before it was torn down. The group includes Veijo, Ines, Veikko and Veli Parviainen, Lasse Peltola, Teuvo Sorvisto, Raili Nuutinen, Kaj Vickträm, Olavi Laine, Toivo Erkkilä, Eelis Viljakainen, and Pentti and Kerttu Hirvonen. (From the collection of Toini Parviainen)

Building bond sold to finance the construction of the new Surprise Lake camp

At the meeting on February 8, 1958, with Väinö Jacobson as chairman, there was discussion of fixing the old camp and building a dance pavilion. Two years later, at the January 17, 1960 meeting it was decided that the old log cabin would be torn down and a new building with a dance pavilion built. In order to raise funds for this project, the club sold 27 building bonds for $10.00 each. Some of these were redeemed starting in 1963, but most were donated to the club.

During the summer of 1960, using the design of Väinö Mäkelä, the new camp was built with Veikko Parviainen and

Pekka Kuisma and Olavi Laine tearing down the old camp at Surprise Lake, winter of 1960 (From the collection of Pekka Kuisma)

Workers, including Pentti Mäkelä, Voitto Ylikorpi, Väinö Jacobson and Arvo Tuomi building the new camp at Surprise Lake in May, 1960 (From the collection of Pentti Junni)

Väinö overseeing the construction.

During 1961 the old sauna was torn down, and one with separate facilities for men and women was built. Mrs. Ruth Kuokkanen was assigned to look into getting hydro for the sauna and the dance pavilion, but this did not happen until the fall of 1962, when the club's finances were in better shape.

In subsequent years the camp was a beehive of activity. It was used not only by Kansallisseura, but also by outside groups during the summer. For example, Finlandia Club, Otava Male Choir, Athletic Club Reipas and Kiikurit Folk Dancers rented it for their dances and picnics. In 1962 Finlandia Club held a winter event at the camp, with ski races and sledding.

In 1962 Toini Jacobson suggested that 80 feet of the shoreline could be sold to raise money, but this idea was rejected. But money was certainly needed for the upkeep of this property. Records show that every year repairs had to be done to the building. Sometimes the steps needed fixing, sometimes it was the roof or the chimney that was leaking. New curtains for the kitchen were considered a necessity, rather than a frivolity. The land was low and tended to be wet, so Erkki Sirén rented a backhoe to dig a ditch to improve

The completed project, March, 1961 – the new Kansallisseura camp (From the collection of Pentti Junni)

Whether it was summer or winter, Kansallisseura members enjoyed a range of activities at Surprise Lake camp.

On the sauna lauteet (benches) in December, 1960: Raili Parviainen wielding a vasta (bath whisk), Ingmar Carlson, Håkan Carlson, Macbud, Kaarina Parviainen and Raimo Mäntysalo, definitely not having a sauna. (From the collection of Erkki Sirén)

the drainage in 1978. At his suggestion a tin roof at a cost of $1200.00 was installed in April, 1991 to end the constant damage caused by the heavy snow. Unfortunately the next winter was particularly hard and the roof again required repairs.

The sauna was also often in need of repairs, proving that it was put to good use by the members. Over the years the floor needed fixing, the *kiuas* (heater) had to be replaced more than once, a new shed was built for firewood, and several new coats of paint were applied. In the 1970s Vic Laurin donated heavy fir timbers to fix the sauna foundation.

The sauna was always the main attraction at the camp, whether it was summer or winter. Members of the Nor-Shor Youth Club often drove to Surprise Lake to enjoy a sauna. The strains of *"Koti-maani ompi Suomi"* ("Finland is My Homeland") could be heard drifting out over the lake as this impromptu choir sat on the *lauteet* (sauna benches) and sang in multi-part harmony. And afterwards, what could be more delicious than sauna *makkara* (sausage) cooked hanging on a large nail, sizzling above the *kiuas*.

A high diving tower was built in 1959 and was a favourite piece of "playground equipment" for the young and the

Pauli Lumiala and Teuvo Sorvisto displaying fine diving form, Juhannus (Midsummer), 1959 (From the collection of Marjatta Ylikorpi)

At Surprise Lake Camp even the winter ice failed to deter these swimmers from taking a dip. Among the hardy souls are: Pertti and Liisa Kaski, Pauli Lumiala, Taisto Miettinen, Veijo Parviainen, Raimo Mäntysalo, Marjatta Lumiala, Raili Parviainen, Reino Erkkilä, Olavi Laine and Erkki Sirén.

not-so-old. Amateurs tested their mettle by jumping off the lower spring board, holding their nose and screaming all the way down. The pros, on the other hand, showed off their style by swan-diving gracefully from the top.

As the years passed, the tower became quite shaky and there was talk of taking it down. No further diving competitions were held after 1967 for safety reasons, but in 1971 the tower was still up, and no decision had been made on whether it should be repaired or removed. Eventually the tower was torn down and a new dock was built.

In the winter a hole was cut in the lake ice, a narrow log was placed across it, and then a whooping, steaming stream of men and women ran out of the sauna and took turns lowering themselves into the icy hole. Brrr! But how warm the winter air felt afterwards!

In 1979 Reino Erkkilä, Pentti Junni and Erkki Sirén were elected trustees of the Surprise Lake Camp, when one of the originals, Niilo Viitala, passed away. By 1980 the camp had increased

Reetta Junni, Anja Nenonen, Sauli and Kerttu Häkkinen on the new dock; Helena and Anja Junni in the water (From the collection of P. Junni)

considerably in value, and the cost of fire insurance and taxes was a concern. Except for the Surprise Lake Swim and the Midsummer dances, there was little "official activity" at the camp.

On August 13, 2001 the Surprise Lake camp was sold. For years the dream of the club had been to have its own home, but in the 1930s the Depression

Pentti Junni locking the door of Surprise Lake camp for the last time on August 12, 2001 (From the collection of Pentti Junni)

had taken its toll on people's finances. In the 1940s the club's money had gone to help the old homeland as it struggled in the throes of war, but finally, in the 1950s, the dream had become a reality.

The Surprise Lake camp was the true heart of Port Arthur Kansallisseura, and during the almost 50 years that the club owned the property, the children and grandchildren of the original members were able to catch fish, enjoy a sauna, swim in the clear waters, or dip into a hole in the ice.

Surely all the members of Kansallisseura were there in spirit, bidding farewell to the beloved place, when Pentti Junni locked the doors for the last time on August 12, 2001.

---

[1] *Canadan Uutiset*, February 21, 1929.

Celebrations

One of the duties of Kansallisseura, as stated in its rules, was to hold patriotic events in the community.

Kalevala Day

On Feb. 28, 1926, only a month after its inception, Kansallisseura organized the very first nationalistic celebration held in Port Arthur—the Kalevala Day. Despite the short planning time, the program was substantial, including opening music by Miss Helmi Lassi, a poem by Mrs. Hilja Korte, a solo by Mrs. Vieno Paananen, a reading by Miss Sanni Kallio, a tone poem by a choir with a soloist, a speech by Mr. Kosti Koivukoski, and a piano solo by Miss Helmi Lassi.

One of the more unusual performances at the 1928 Kalevala Day celebration was "*Ma oksalla ylimmällä*" ("Here on the Highest Branch") played by Mr. Kanto on a saw. This was so well received by the large audience that he had to give an encore, and repeat the performance at another event later in the year.

Kansallisseura celebrated the Kalevala Centenary in a church on February 28, 1935 with a very distinguished program of speeches, poetry and music. In the first ten years of its existence Kansallisseura organized at least four

Photograph of Elias Lönnrot from the Kansallisseura archives, with an edition of The Kalevala *from 1944 (Courtesy of Veikko Parviainen)*

Kalevala Day festivities. After 1935 this event was taken over by other organizations, with Kansallisseura only participating in the performances. For example, in 1949 the young brothers, Onni and Väinö Jacobson Jr., played the piano and sang.

Independence Day

At the first Independence Day celebration held by Kansallisseura on December 6, 1926, Consul A.J. Jalkanen from Duluth was invited to be a guest speaker. The Independence Day program in 1929 was distinguished and diverse. There were several speeches, which were a great favourite with the audience. Mr. Eric Korte and Mr. K. Justin spoke, as well as Mr. Gibbon, the mayor of Port Arthur and, of course, Mr. Koivukoski. The admission of 25¢ generated 1,145 :- (Finn markkas) for *Suomen Yhdistyneille Koteja Kodittomille Lapsille* (Homes for the Homeless Children) fund. This organization, renamed *Pelastakaa Lapset r.y.* (Save the Children) in the 1940s, became the traditional recipient of Kansallisseura Independence Day profits.

On December 7, 1930 Kansallisseura celebrated its most successful Independence Day, when an estimated 500 people crammed the Sons of England Hall to overflowing. The hall was decorated tastefully with large and small Finnish flags. On one wall on a white background the words "FINLANDIA REDIVIVA" (Finland reborn) were worked with evergreen branches. Overall, the program was dignified and varied, and included three speeches. Mr. Kosti Koivukoski spoke on the ups and downs of Finland since its independence, Mr. Emil Seppälä compared the destiny of Finland with that of Israel, and Lieutenant-Colonel Francis Milton brought out the similarity between Canada and Finland as young nations forged by war. He expressed his pleasure that loyal Finns can be counted among the best citizens of this country.

A reporter from *Port Arthur News Chronicle*, who was present at this function, was obviously impressed by all he saw and heard. In an editorial on December 9, he defended Port Arthur Finns who had been accused of playing a significant role in serious disturbances in October[1], which had led to an increase in the city's police force. *Canadan Uutiset* reported on the article under the headline "*Canadalainen lehti antaa tunnuksen valkoisille suomalaisille.*"[2] (Canadian newspaper gives recognition to White Finns.) The *News Chronicle* reporter refuted the accusation of alleged Finnish participation in the October disturbances, by listing the many positive contributions of Finns in the area.

Article from Canadan Uutiset *of December 11, 1930, reporting on a* Port Arthur News Chronicle *article extolling the virtues of Finns*

"The extra police force, which was recruited last October, included sixty Finns, of whom 95% were unemployed at the time. Finns have participated actively in many of the recent public undertakings, such as the building of the new general hospital. Young Finns are among the most hard-working and advanced students in the city's schools.

The results of Finnish perseverance can also be seen in the countryside. Especially in Gorham they have performed miracles in transforming unproductive soil into fertile farmlands. They have created fruitful lands from areas that almost any other nationality would have rejected as useless.

Anyone, who considers the average Canadian Finn a Red, because of a few loud agitators, does not understand the true nature of these hard-working and interesting people."

The above is an example of how patriotic activities helped to improve the reputation and image of Finns in Canada.

In 1932 and 1934 the Independence Day celebrations were co-organized by Kansallisseura and the church. It was not until 1943 that Kansallisseura again held Independence Day on its own.

The 20th Independence Day was celebrated at the Sons of England Hall on December 6, 1937. Kansallisseura members assisted with, but did not organize the program. Mr. Koivukoski was the Master of Ceremonies, the women of Kansallisseura served coffee, and the club's young men gathered the usual collection. The program had three speeches, as well as music by an orchestra, choir singing, solos by Mrs. Paananen and Mrs. Vera Jacobson, a cello solo by Miss Morrison, a violin solo by G. Wickström, poetry by O. Vainio, piano solos by Miss Dora Alanen, Miss Kathleen Paananen and Mr. Armas Laakso, a piano duet by Miss Dora Alanen and A. Rantanen, and solo dancing by "little Finnish girl Eleanor Rae who...amazed and delighted the audience with her gymnastic dancing." [3]

On Independence Day, 1941, when Kansallisseura seemed to be dormant, Mr. Koivukoski held a party for his friends at his Pohjola Cafe. He spoke to them about "Aino". Curiously, considering that at this time Finland was fighting for its very life, no record could be found of any official Independence Day celebration by any club in Port Arthur.

It is also strange that the re-awakened Kansallisseura held only a social evening, instead of an Independence Day celebration on Sunday, December 6, 1942. Admission to this event was free, and the evening went *"verrattain hyvin"* (reasonably well). The collection was used to cover the evening's expenses, and was *not* sent to Homes for the Homeless Children, as had been the tradition. However, Mr. Koivukoski did speak on the subject of Finnish independence *"...koska iltama sattui Suomen itsenäisyyspäivän päälle."* (...since the social happened to fall on the Finnish Independence Day.)[4]

Starting on December 5, 1943, and for the next six years, Kansallisseura once again took over the organization of the Finnish Independence Day celebrations. In an article called *"Kansallisseuran kuulumisia"* ("News of Kansallisseura"), *Canadan Uutiset* described the event at Sons of England Hall in great detail. *"Ohjelma aloitettiin Kansallisseuran omaksuman tavan mukaan yhteisesti laulamalla Sillanpään Marssilaulun."* (The program was opened with the singing of "Marching Song" by Sillanpää, which has been adopted by Kansallisseura as a tradition.)[5]

The 80th birthday of Jean Sibelius in 1945 was combined by Kansallisseura with the Independence Day celebrations. On December 4 at the Sons of England Hall, a congratulatory telegram was sent to Mr. Sibelius from all the people attending the event. The telegram contained the following text:

Telegram sent to Jean Sibelius on his 80th birthday in 1945, with a photo of The Master from the Kansallis-seura archives

"Professor Jean Sibelius,
Sibelius Celebration,
Helsinki:
A group of several hundred nationalistic Finns in Port Arthur, Canada, gathered at a Finnish Independence Day celebration organized by the local Kansallisseura, has dedicated the event to your 80th birthday in recognition of the great work you have done during your long life on behalf of Finland and its people. The group thus sends you heartfelt congratulations, as well as the hope that the Creator will grant you many more happy and pleasant years of life. Long live the Great Son of a small nation! Long live the King of Music of Finland and of the whole world!"

Canadan Uutiset also reported that the performers "*...antoi yleisölle hiotun ja täysipainoisen tuotteen*" (...gave the audience a polished and full-measured performance) that included a children's orchestra conducted by Mr. Cheetham.[6]

In 1947 Finland had been independent for 30 years and to mark this auspicious day, the celebrations were very festive. In fact, people were asked to remove their coats so as to give the occasion a more dignified aura. The standing-room-only event raised over $100.00 and was very well received. The program included a melodrama as well as songs by the Otava Mixed Choir.

The 1948 celebration generated a profit of $53.49, and every penny of that was sent to the Swedish American Line for the purchase of a 145-pound bag of green coffee. M/S *Tunaholm* sailed from Pier 95, North River, in New York City to Helsinki on April 15 of the following year and delivered the coffee to *Pelastakaa Lapset r.y.*

Norma Ristimäki at the piano, with Helmi Tolvanen, Ellen Poutanen, Esteri Albrecht, Vera Jacobson, Edith Saasto and Aamor Albrecht, 1951 Independence Day (Photo from Kansallisseura archives)

Kansallisseura Independence Day celebrations, circa 1951. According to an accompanying hand-written scrap of paper, the men are "Koivugaski, Majuri Vilson and Tengakka". (Photo from Kansallisseura archives)

SWEDISH AMERICAN LINE

600 DORCHESTER STREET WEST • MONTREAL 2, QUE.

TELEPHONE
PLATEAU 9051

CARL E. WASELIUS
DISTRICT MANAGER

April 26, 1949.

Mr. K. Koivukoski,
65 B So. Cumberland St.,
Port Arthur, Ont.

Dear Mr. Koivukoski:

Referring to our letter of February 7, and to our conversation while the writer visited Port Arthur, in connection with the shipment of green coffee to "Pelastakaa Lapset r.y." in Helsinki, we are quoting below a letter received from our New York Office, under date of April 22, which speaks for itself:

"Referring to your letters of February 1, March 25 and April 5, we were pleased to advise that we purchased, through our port steward, one bag of 145 lbs of green coffee from the well-known firm of Seeman Brothers, Inc. of "White Rose" fame. The bag of coffee was placed in charge of the of our M/S "Tunaholm" which sailed from New York, April 15 through to Helsinki, Finland where the bag will be turned over to Victor Ek's office for the disposal by "Pelastakaa Lapset r.y.". The cash discount was accepted as part compensation for the discount in Canadian dollars.

Kindly notify Mr. Koivukoski of the shipment so that he will communicate with Victor Ek's office in order to obtain delivery."

It is noted that our New York Office has left out a word on the fifth line of the above quotation between the words the and of, but it is presumed that this should be either the chief officer or chief steward.

Very truly yours,

SWEDISH AMERICAN LINE.

Per: [signature]

CEW/SH
Encl.
P.S. We are enclosing herewith a receipted bill from Seeman Brothers, Inc. in New York.

Letter from Swedish American Line, reporting that coffee, purchased with Independence Day profits, had been sent to Finland to Pelastakaa Lapset r.y.

At a meeting on November 11, 1949 Independence Day festivities were discussed, but the event never took place. Likewise in 1950 it was the Red Cross that held the celebrations on December 3. The church held theirs on the sixth, and although Kansallisseura did not participate, Mr. Koivukoski gave a speech.

Kansallisseura, together with the Finnish Aid Society and the Historical Society, celebrated Independence Day in 1951. No record of participation by Kansallisseura in any Independence Day celebrations was found past 1953.

Anniversaries

Besides the patriotic festivities, Kansallisseura marked its anniversaries with special events. The nationalistic tone and dignity at these occasions fully matched those of the Independence and Kalevala Day celebrations. The club's fourth anniversary on April 16, 1930 was the first for which records exist. *Canadan Uutiset*[7] gave a description of the program. To open the festivities, "*Vaasan Marssi*" was sung, accompanied by Mr. Armas Laakso on the accordion. The opening speech by Mr. Lauri Kovalainen was followed by a piano solo by Miss Kathleen Paananen, a poem by Mr. Ilmari Jolkka, a solo by Mr. Kosti Koivukoski, choir music, a speech by Mr. Koivukoski, a solo by Mrs. Maria Paananen and a piano solo by Mr. Armas Laakso. On a lighter note, Mr. Koivukoski sang some comical songs, and the program ended with folk dancing by a group which had received $6.78 from the club for their new outfits. This was followed by general dancing to the music of Armas Laakso Orchestra.

On the club's fifth anniversary on April 21, 1931, a congratulatory letter arrived from the Central Organization of Loyal Finns in Canada (COLFC), which had been established the previous year by *Toronton Suomalainen Kansallisseura*. Despite much debate, the Port Arthur club had yet to join it. The quaint and ornamental wording of the letter is typical of the era and possibly the flattering tone was an attempt to persuade the oldest Kansallisseura in Canada to join the central organization.

"Honoured Club members,
For five long years you have toiled at your trail-blazing work; opened the track on behalf of Finnishness and humanity; laboured in an exemplary manner. We request to be included among the well-wishers and wish you continued enthusiasm and sacrifice. It is gratifying to see that among Finns one can still find people who have the stamina and enthusiasm to volunteer on behalf of the whole Finnish immigrant population. Long live Port Arthur Kansallisseura.
Toronto, Ontario, April, 1931
COLFC and on behalf of Toronto Finnish Kansallisseura;
Lauri Salmio, Chairman"

At this event Mr. Kosti Koivukoski, the club's chairman since its inception, was installed as an Honorary Chairman. The program consisted of the following performances:[8]

Speech – Mr. K. Koivukoski
Speech – Mayor Ibbetson
Opening music – Mrs. Helmi Lassi
Poem – O. Järvelä
Solo – Mrs. Vera Jacobson, accompanied by Mrs. Hill
Quartet – "Poor Boy" and "Iceland"
Dance – Six girls
Violin solo – G. Wickström, accompanied by Mr. Armas Laakso
Solo – Mrs. Maria Paananen, accompanied by Miss K. Paananen
Piano solo – Mr. Armas Laakso
Quartet – "By the Fountain", "Bright Star" and "Dear Finland"
Piano duet – Miss Kathleen Paananen and Miss Hilkka Arnio

Port -Arthurin Kansallisseura,
Port-Arthur.Ont.

Arv,Seuran jäsenet;

Uraa uurtavaa työtä olette jo viisi pitkää vuotta tehneet,olette latua aukaisseet,Suomalaisuuden ja ihmisyyden puolesta olette esimerkillisellä tavalla työtä tehneet.Pyydäm me yhtyä onnittelijoiden joukkoon ja toivomme jatkuvaa intoa ja uhrautuvaisuutta. On ilahuttavaa nähdä että vielä löytyy Suomalaisissa henkilöitä jotka jaksavat innostua ja jotka jak savat tehdä palkatonta työtä koko Suomalaisen siirtolais heimon hyväksi. Kauan eläköön Port-Arthurin Kansallisseura.

Toronto,Ont, Huhtikuulla, 1931.

Central Organization of Loyal Finns
in Canada.
sekä
Toronton Suomalaisen Kansallisseuran
puolesta;   *Lauri Salmia*
                   P;johtaja.

Letter received from COLFC and Toronton Suomalainen Kansallisseura *on Port Arthur Kansallisseura's 5th anniversary*

The seventh anniversary was marked on May 16, 1933 with moderate success. It is likely that no celebrations were held on the 10th anniversary in 1936, since the club was then essentially dormant. It is surprising, however, that no celebrations were recorded in 1946 for the 20th year. Perhaps the club was too busy with their fundraising for Finland.

The 30th anniversary celebrations on May 19, 1956 were quite problematic. Two years previously the club had purchased the Surprise Lake camp and had only 17 paid members. Since they had little money and there were too few members to put together a program, letters asking for support were sent to Sudbury Kansallisseura and COLFC in Montreal (which Port Arthur had finally joined in 1933, abandoned in the late 1930s, and re-joined in 1954). Unfortunately, at this time COLFC was busy with preparations for the Finnish Canadian Grand Festival in Montreal and could not offer much help. After much correspondence, the Sudbury Sampo girls and boys came to perform, and were sent a cheque for $50.00 to cover their travel expenses. As the keynote speaker, COLFC recommended Mr. Volu Varpio from Sudbury, who ended his informative speech with these rousing words:

mieleeni että seuran jäsen-
määrä oli melko pieni verrattuna
suureen suomalais asutukseen
paikkakunnalla.
Tämä [illegible] havainnoitsijan
silmään kuuluu että vähän on
ollut heitään laista suuren ylei-
sön myötämielisyys Kalevaiseen
työhön ja sen tekijöihin. Sitä
suurenemalla kunnioituksella
seuraan toimihenkilöiden sit-
keyttä ylläpitää seuraa edelleen.
Jatkakaa yhä työtän-
ne ja kasvakoon seuranne sanan
vain 30 vuoden aikana suureksi
tiedon ja opin puuksi jota on
täytetty ilon, menestyksen ja onnen
oksilla, kaunan, rakkauden ja yksi-
mielisyyden kukkasilla.
Kunnioitan tätä 30 vuotta toimineiden
toimitsijoiden työtä seuraavasti:
I
Ole kova niinkuin rauta.
Itse itseäsi auta,
Eessäs elo taikka hauta.
II
Itse vastaa elos vaali
Korkealle olkoon maalis,
Tunto tyyni työsi saalis.
Tiedän tuntamme tyyneyden
30 vuotiselta työ-taipaleelta.
Onnittelen seuraa juhlapäivä-
nä ja sen jäseniä. Korkein synnyin-
maatamme ja Canadaa suojelee
Veljeydellä Vohi Varpio.

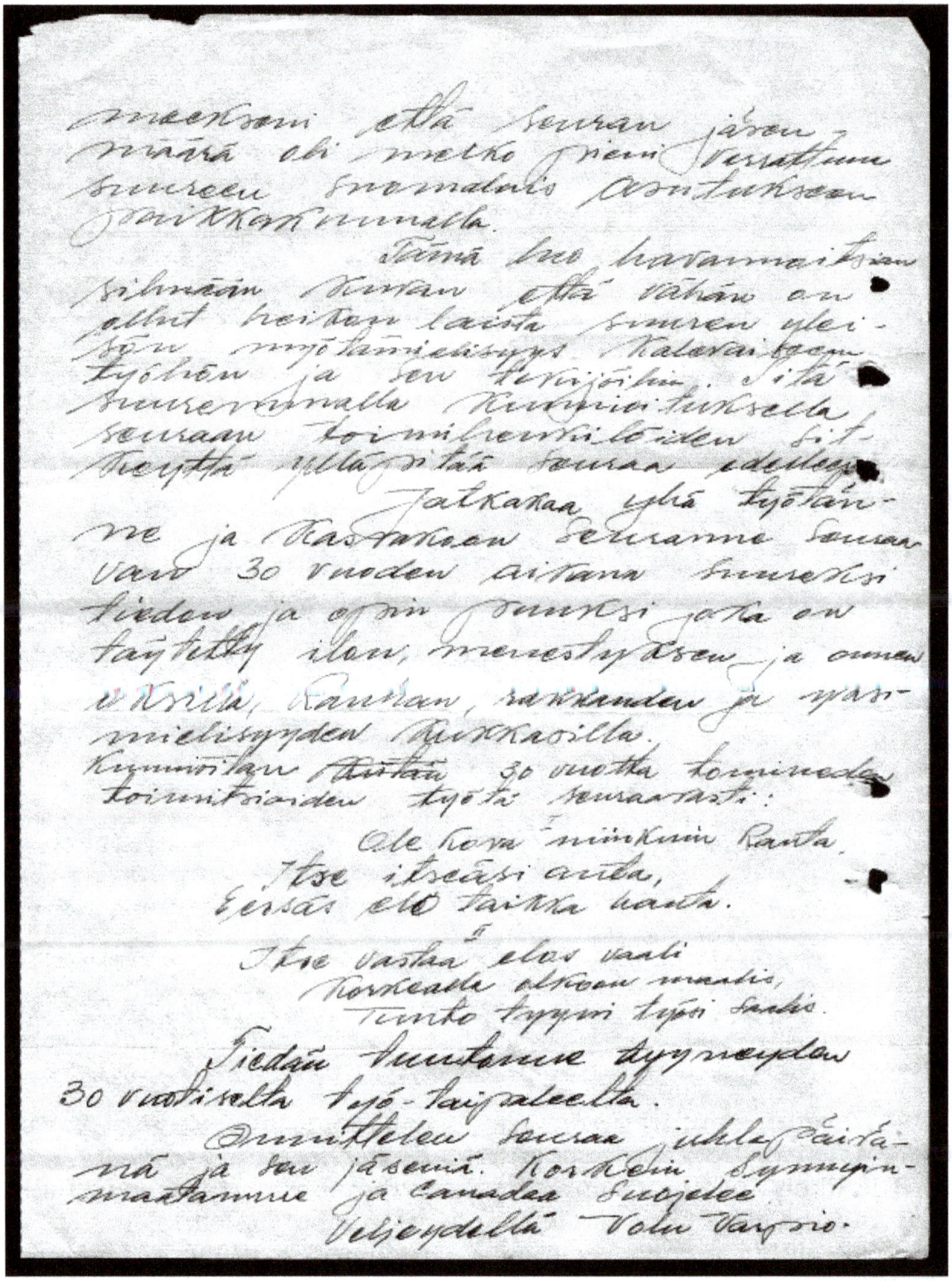

The ending of Mr. Varpio's keynote address at Port Arthur Kansallisseura's 30th anniversary celebrations in 1956

"Continue your work and let your organization grow during the next 30 years into a grand tree of knowledge and learning, filled with branches of joy, success and happiness, and flowers of peace, love and unity. I honour those who have laboured for 30 years with these words:

I
Be hard as iron,
Be self-reliant,
Whether you face life or death.

II
Be responsible for your life
Place your goal high,
Thus you will procure peace of mind.

Honouring your peace of mind after 30 years of labour.

I congratulate the club and its members on this anniversary. Lord on High protect our homeland and Canada.

In brotherhood, Volu Varpio."

Kansallisseura received several congratulatory telegrams, as well as a certificate from COLFC honouring their "...trail-blazing cultural work in the nationalistic labour arena for the last thirty years."

At the end of the evening Kauko Kiviluoma Orchestra provided music for the dancing. The admission price of 60¢ netted the club a $70.43 profit.

The 40th anniversary was celebrated on October 23, 1966 at the Finlandia Club with the following program:

"40th Anniversary Celebration.

'O Canada'
Opening speech by Maino Mannila
'You Are Our Dearest Land' sung by the audience
Choir singing by Oras Mixed Choir
Choral speaking by Women of Kaleva
Solo by Taina Leskelä
Folk dancing by Kansallisseura Young People
Speech by Pentti Junni

Certificate received from Canadan Lojaalisten Suomalaisten Liitto *(Central Organization of Loyal Finns in Canada) on Port Arthur Kansallisseura's 30th anniversary in 1956*

```
                PORT ARTHURIN SUOMALAINEN KANSALLISSEURA.

        Perustettu 20 pv. Tammikuuta 1926. Rekisteröity nimellä
        The Loyal Finns in Canada.

                        40v. Juhla.

                O'CANADA..............
                Tervehdyssanat......... M.Jannila
                Yhteislaulu........... Olet Maamme Armahin,-
                Kuorolaulua........... Sekakuoro ORAS
                Lausuntaryhmä......... Kalevan Naiset
                Yksinlaulua........... Taina Leskelä
                Kansantanhuja......... Kansallisseuran Nuorisoryhmä
                Puhe ................. P.Junni
                        - Väliaika -
                Kuorolaulua........... Mieskuoro OTAVA
                Lausuntaa............. Inkeri Mäkelä
                Viulusooloja.......... Yvonne Olsson , säest.D.Dahlgren
                                       Slavanic Dance no.2 in E minor
                                       sävelt änyt Dvorak
                                       Polish Dance. by Severn
                Duettolaulua.......... Eeva Sora, Pentti Junni
                Hanurinsoittoa........ Trio
                Maamme -
```

Program for Port Arthur Kansallisseura's 40th anniversary in 1966

Intermission

Choir singing by Otava Male Choir
Recital by Inkeri Mäkelä
Violin solo by Yvonne Olsson, accompanied by D. Dahlgren
Duet by Eeva Sora and Pentti Junni
Accordion solo by Trio
Finnish National Anthem"

Founding members invited to the event were Mrs. Irene Suline, Mr. and Mrs. Eeli Hendrickson, Mrs. Vera Jacobson, Mr. Leonard W. Mäki, Mr. Niilo Kyrö and Mrs. Vieno Rita. Honorary members present were Mr. and Mrs. Ralph Poutanen, Mr. Aarne Rita, Mr. and Mrs. Niilo Viitala, Mrs. Tyyne Karttunen, Mrs. Matilda Tuomi and Mr. and Mrs. Väinö Jacobson. Congratulatory telegrams were received from the COLFC in Sudbury,

Photo of Topi Jousmäki Orchestra playing the opening march, with the Kansallisseura executive and honorary members seated in front of the stage at Port Arthur Kansallisseura's 50th anniversary

Sudbury Kansallisseura, Knights of Kaleva Sampo Maja 51, and one from many former Kansallisseura members in Toronto.

Although Port Arthur Kansallisseura existed until 2002, the 50th anniversary, on Oct. 2, 1976, was the last recorded milestone formally celebrated with a dinner-dance at Finlandia Club. Reino Erkkilä, Master of Ceremonies for the evening, introduced those founding and honorary members who were present. Pentti Junni, the club's long-time chairman, spoke on the history of the organization and on its activities from its beginning in 1926 to present time. Flower arrangements were received from Athletic Club Reipas, Women's Choir Oras, Otava Male Choir, Violet Florist, Ostrobothnian Club, Finlandia Club and the Women of Kaleva. Telegrams arrived from Ambassador Niilo Pusa, Sudbury and Montreal Kansallisseuras, as well as one from former Kansallisseura members in Toronto.

By the time the 60th anniversary rolled around in 1986, Kansallisseura's annual activity consisted mainly of a couple of dances and the Surprise Lake Swim with lunch. No discussion of any anniversary event was found. In 1996, on the club's 70th anniversary year, the last Midsummer dance marked the end of all formal social activity.

In addition to its own celebrations, members of Kansallisseura often helped other clubs at important events held in Port Arthur, such as the Jean Sibelius Centennial Concert on December 4, 1965, organized by the Central Committee of Finnish Societies.

Program and ticket for Jean Sibelius Centennial Concert, Coliseum, December 4, 1965

---

[1] Ahti Tolvanen, *Finntown, A Perspective on Urban Integration, Port Arthur Finns in the Inter-war Period: 1918 – 1939,* (University of Helsinki, Finn Forum, 1984) p. 61.
[2] *Canadan Uutiset,* December 11, 1930.
[3] *Canadan Uutiset,* December 12, 1937.
[4] *Canadan Uutiset,* December 9, 1942.
[5] *Canadan Uutiset,* December 16, 1943.
[6] *Canadan Uutiset,* December 12, 1945.
[7] *Canadan Uutiset,* April 24, 1930.
[8] *Canadan Uutiset,* April 29, 1931.

Culture

Rule 3(c) of Loyal Finns in Canada exhorted the branches to "establish within the club theatre, music, sport, discussion, etc. groups, and in this manner give the members an opportunity to develop both their physical and spiritual abilities."

Choirs

Finns are known as "*laulava kansa*" (singing nation) and thus it is not surprising that a mixed choir was one of the first organizations Mr. Kosti Koivukoski launched after arriving in Port Arthur in 1925. Immediately following this, he helped to establish the Port Arthur Kansallisseura. It was a logical step for the choir to join the new club, and so by the end of February, 1926, it was practicing under the Kansallisseura banner. The choir performed for the first time on March 10, 1926 at the *alkajaisjuhla* (opening ceremony), the first official social event of the new Kansallisseura. It sang two songs and received "*myrskyiset suosionosoitukset*" (stormy applause).

Although the choir often performed at the social events put on by the organization, it was not until the meeting on March 06, 1932 that the club decided to pay the $5.00 hall rental fee for its rehersals. The first recorded mention of the choir under the name, Sointu, was at the social evening on May 5, 1932. A few days later Sointu gave a very successful concert, which was called "one of the best concerts in ages". Throughout 1932 and 1933 Sointu was very active and even received mention in an article in the Finnish periodical *Suomen Kuvalehti*.

In 1934 the choir was again on the pages of *Suomen Kuvalehti* in an article on the 50th anniversary of the city of Port Arthur. However, choir activity seems to have slowed down somewhat around this time, because in its April 11, 1934 edition *Canadan Uutiset* reported that Sointu choir was awake again and had their first practice that day. But the "awakening" doesn't seem to have lasted, because during 1936 and 1937 there were no more references to Sointu. Instead *Canadan Uutiset* sometimes wrote, under "Ecclesiastical Activities", about a mixed choir (probably containing some ex-Sointu members) led by Mr. Koivukoski. For example, on April 12, 1936 it reported that "...about 30 members of the Port Arthur mixed choir performed for the first time in their new black outfits in the church."

No further reference to Sointu was found in *Canadan Uutiset* until May 14, 1941, when Mr. Koivukoski urged former members of Sointu choir to come to an

Picture from a 1932 issue of Suomen Kuvalehti *of Sointu Choir and Mr. K. Koivukoski*

important meeting. Presumably the choir revival again failed, because that was the last reference found for Sointu. But throughout 1942, 1943 and 1944 there are references to a *"tilapäinen"* (temporary) choir, usually described as being "small" or "made up of 15 singers", which participated at various Kansallisseura events. Perhaps these were the remaining Sointu members still performing for the love of singing.

But Sointu was not the only choir found in the long history of Kansallisseura. The minutes of the meeting on December 27, 1929 contain a discussion on starting a female choir. The task was left to *Käsityökerho* (Needlecraft Club), but nothing came of this plan. However, a highlight of the very successful Independence Day celebration on December 7, 1930 was the male choir, which sang songs it had been practicing specifically for this event. *Canadan Uutiset* on December 11 reported: *"Erikoinen maininta annettakoon myös suomalaisesta mieskuorosta, joka vasta lyhyen aikaa harjoitelleena on päässyt hyvin lupaaviin tuloksiin"* (Special mention should be given also to the Finnish male choir which, after practicing for only a short time, has achieved very promising results.) The choir, as usual, was led by Mr. Koivukoski. The male choir continued to appear at various Kansallisseura events, such as the social evening on November 7, 1933, but by 1937 all references to it were only under the "Ecclesiastical Activities" in the newspaper.

Although there were no other choirs that performed under Kansallisseura, the history of the Otava choir has a number of admittedly tenuous links to the club. The first link was the fact that the choir was started by Mr. Kosti Koivukoski in a meeting on April 5, 1938. He wanted to put together a mixed choir of about 60 singers, and felt that in order to reach that number, it could not be limited to any one club. A month later the choir performed for the first time at a Rotary International Festival, where "...*se esitti jotakuinkin huomattavaa ansiokkuutta*" (...it exhibited somewhat noteworthy effort). The first mention of the choir's name as Otava was found in a *Canadan Uutiset* article in August of 1938.

The second link to Kansallisseura was the fact that many of the singers in the mixed Otava choir were former members of Sointu. In 1950 Mr. Koivukoski turned 60, and decided to stop conducting Otava. The choir seems to have gone into a temporary hiatus, and it was at this point that the final link to Kansallisseura occurred.

In 1951 there was a spike in the number of immigrants to Canada from Finland, many of them settling in Port Arthur. On June 16 Kansallisseura held a social event where recent immigrants were asked to perform. *Canadan Uutiset* of June 27 reported that "...a male choir, led by K. Koivukoski, let ring out two beautiful songs. Let us raise our hats on behalf of the people of Port Arthur to you, male choir, and don't leave your candle under a bushel, but let it shine to bring joy to people." It was also at this event that "...Erkki Kuokkanen had come from Finland and said greetings, people of Port Arthur, and smiled so beautifully. I thought that here comes someone special, and so it was." The male choir did continue, just as the newspaper had beseeched. On April 16, 1952, conducted by Ruth Kuokkanen, Otava sang as a male choir at another Kansallisseura event. And the rest, as they say, is history.

Discussion and Debating Club

Information on the Kansallisseura Discussion and Debating Club that flourished in 1929, can be found in several interesting articles in *Canadan Uutiset*. The following undated article from the club's files gives a summary of its aims and activities in the early days.

"A new undertaking has been added to Kansallisseura's activities—namely a Discussion and Debating Club which has already met, and which will be held on a regular basis—at least for the time being—every Sunday afternoon at

Article from Canadan Uutiset *in 1929 on the aims and advantages of the Debating club*

3:00 p.m. These events are both useful and refreshing, as some subject of general interest is taken under discussion—something that is close to the lives of Finns in Canada. Thus their horizons are broadened, their knowledge of today's important events increased, and at the same time they learn to express their opinions without useless shyness or timidity. On the other hand, since these meetings are meant mainly for club members and those planning to join, we get to know each other better and share the feeling that we all belong to a great Finnish family...In between more serious discussions, lighter fare, such as poems, jokes, etc. is presented to keep the atmosphere lively and joyful. Judging by the active participation by the numerous attendees at the first two meetings, we can conclude that they will become events to which we will hasten eagerly, and from which we will depart hoping that the week will pass quickly, so we can meet again."

The lively conversation topics included everything from the voyages of Christopher Columbus to the flight of Charles Lindberg, as well as more intellectual and idealistic subjects, such as the spiritual needs of nationalistic Finns in Canada. Often these meetings lasted for several hours and included the singing of beautiful Finnish folk songs.

Sometimes the discussion centered on the burning question of finding a home for Kansallisseura. One such meeting lasted for three hours and was changed from a Debating Club meeting to an official General Meeting, because so many members were present and the interest in the topic was so great.

Many members were generous in opening their homes to the Debating Club and providing refreshments for this large group. Records show that among them were Mr. and Mrs. Aleksi Lassi, Mrs. A. Hammarberg and Mrs. Ida Virtanen.

According to *Canadan Uutiset*, in 1929 the Debating Club took a summer recess, and never seems to have resumed its activity. Perhaps it was felled by the Depression, when men had to go and find work wherever it was available.

Library and Publications

By October 1933 Kansallisseura was operating a library containing a few books donated by members. Mrs. Milja Järvinen volunteered to look after it. On January 21, 1934 a *lukurengas* (reading circle) was set up in order to raise money to buy more books for the library. Members paid 25¢ to be the first to read a new book, after which it went to general circulation. On November 6, 1934 a social evening was held in support of the library. Admission was 25¢ and Mr. Kosti Koivukoski spoke about his trip to Finland. After 1935 there was no further mention of the library, which appears to have been discontinued.

In 1931 Kansallisseura decided to print publications on a regular basis to provide Finnish reading material for the members. One of these was *Kalevalainen Kansa* (*People of Kaleva*), a monthly publication. The first edition was published by Mr. Lauri Kovalainen in March, 1931, with the next edition by Mrs. Tyyne Mäki and Mrs. Helen Pelkonen. The paper received profuse thanks from the chairman for its interesting and informative content. The last recorded issue of this newspaper was published by Mr. Toivo Puuska and Mr. Emil Suuronen, but no copies of *Kalevalainen Kansa* could be found.

Siirtolainen (*The Immigrant*), an annual publication that allowed people to express their ideas anonymously, was published for 1933 Christmas reading.

The one existing copy contains editorials about the Finnish community, sentimental stories about immigrants, and Christmas greetings from individuals and businesses in Port Arthur. The following is a sampling of its contents:

Front page of Siirtolainen *magazine from 1934*

"*Ladun Hiihtäjä*" ("Trail Blazer") - an editorial about the community. The writer feels Kansallisseura's activities have been misunderstood.

"*Valhe*" ("The Lie") - a sentimental tale of lost love, alcoholism, jail, a dying mother and, finally, a reconciliation with the lost love.

"*Vanhojen Tervakantojen Parissa*" ("Among Old Codgers") - an interesting interview with Jaakko Vilhem Harri, who at 86, was one of the oldest Finns in Port Arthur. He had come there in 1879, when there was no town and only four Finns: Harri, Erkkilä, Ainali and Johnson.

"*Kotimaan rannat*" ("Native Shores") - a sentimental tale about Canadian and American Finns going to Russia on a boat. One man, who used to be White, sees the Finnish shore and starts to regret his decision to go to Russia. He gets off the boat, reaches Finland, marries a *Lotta* (a member of women's auxiliary services), and lives happily ever after.

"*Tie Elämään*" ("Road to Life") - an inspirational article about having a goal in life, and correcting those erroneous ways that are preventing you from reaching it.

"*Joulupuuki*" (sic) ("Santa Claus") - a sentimental story about a poor young man who plays Santa Claus and wins a rich girl.

Since singing was part of many Finnish social events, it was suggested at the meeting on March 21, 1926, that a song book should be obtained for the club's use. Eventually Kansallisseura did

Article from April 20, 1944 issue of Canadan Uutiset *on the upcoming Sing Song*

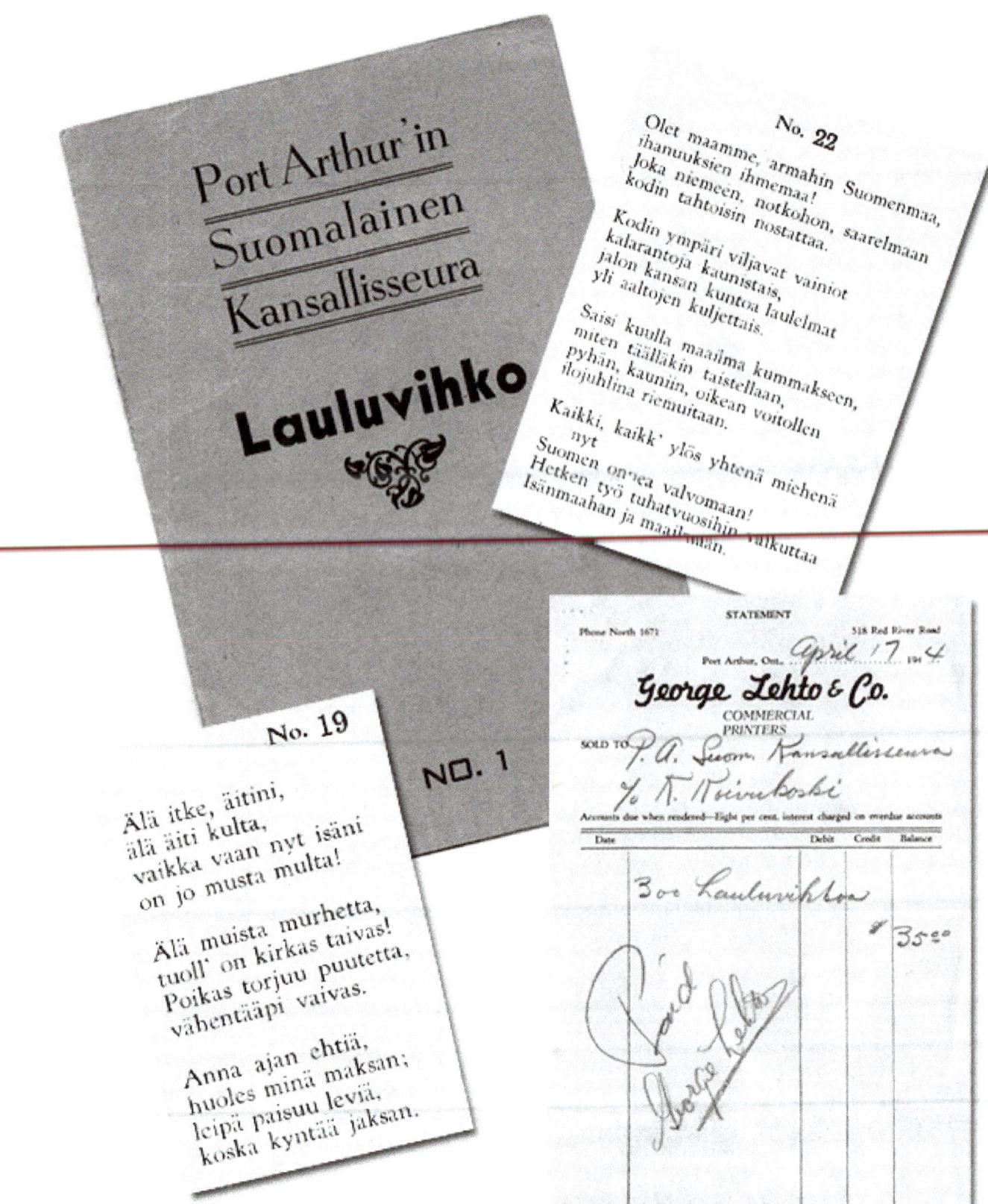

Cover of Lauluvihko (Songbook) *published in 1944 by Kansallisseura, with a statement from George Lehto, the printer, and a small sampling of the kind of music people enjoyed singing*

publish two different song books. One of them, *Kansallisseuran laululipasto* (*Kansallisseura Music Chest*), was a single mimeographed sheet of Finnish clan songs: "*Hämäläisten laulu*", "*Karjalaisten laulu*", "*Savolaisten laulu*" and "*Vaasan Marssi*". The second was a little green booklet, *Lauluvihko No.1* (*Song Book No.1*), printed by George Lehto Press, and was used for the first time on April 24, 1944 at a Sing Song, where the book could be bought for 25¢, or handed back at the end of the evening. According to financial records, 40 copies of the book were sold at this event.

"Once again something new and special is happening at Kansallisseura; something that we Finns haven't tried to do yet, at least not in this community. It is an evening of singing. Canadians have them often and call them 'Sing Song Evenings'. Since we Finns are a 'singing nation', why should we not also organize such an event! And so we shall—on the 24th of this month. At that time we will gather at Sons of England Hall and sing Finnish songs together, all kinds of old familiar songs we used to sing in Finland. Many of us have already forgotten the words to many of the songs, but that fact doesn't need to scare anyone. Kansallisseura has printed a booklet where the words can be found. That booklet will be used for the first time on Monday, the 24th of this month. So all who love songs from the 'old country' should come to the Kansallisseura social evening.

After we have sung ourselves hoarse, we will dance around the floor to the music of an orchestra."

"Despite the rainy weather, the Kansallisseura Sing Song last Monday evening was a success. This was the first attempt of its kind in these parts, which is probably why people found it a bit strange. ...We had time for about twenty songs, and since everyone held a booklet

Article from April 27, 1944 issue of Canadan Uutiset *on the success of the Sing Song evening*

of songs, the singing went well. Numerous booklets were sold, but there are some still available at K. Koivukoski's office. Free booklets can be picked up at the same location by those who donated money for the production of the booklet."

Another Sing Song was held in November, after which the idea seems to have lost steam for a couple of decades. However, in 1963 the club again began to hold a number of Sing Songs, which may have been similar to the ones in 1944, but no further information about them could be found.

At *Kevättempaus -70* (Spring Fling-1970) the audience participated in a Sing-Along using a printed sheet of lyrics provided by Kansallisseura. The choice of music shows the change from the patriotic and melodramatic songs of earlier days to lighter faire. The evening also included a short comedy called *"Kosimassa"* ("The Proposal").

Näytelmä, I os. pilailu KOSIMASSA.

henkilöt:

MAIJU talon tytär – Anja Nenonen
MARI piika – Eeva Mäkelä
JAAKKO isäntä – Pentti Junni
AAPELI – Arto Elonen
SANTERI puhemies – Osmo Mäkeläinen

VANHA MERIMIES MUISTELEE.

Hän oli maata monta nähnyt, oli itää ja etelää.
Oli synnyinmaa unhoon jo jäänyt, ei tuntenut ikävää.
Hän oli kaikissa laivoissa tuttu; Oli niissä kuin kotonaan.
Hän oli seilannut tyynet ja tuuliset veet, kuin mies konsanaan.

Mutt' sitten sattui laiva kerran Idän satamaan saapumaan.
Sitä katseli hän hetken verran, oli tuttu se muodoltaan.
Syömmessä silloin niin kummasti liikkui lipun oman kun nähdä sai.
Oli värit sen vaaleahheet, harmaat ja haaleaheet, vaan tuttu kai.

Tervehdys saapui sieltä kaukaa, hänen rakkailta rannoiltaan.
Hän muisti taas pitkästä aikaa tuon armahan syntymämaan.
Siell' oli rannalla mökki niin harmaa alla tuuhean petäjäpuun.
silloin kyyneleet poskilleen vierimään sai ja hän unhotti kaiken muun.

Villiruusu.

On metsän siimeksessä pien villiruusunen,-
sen salon sydämmessä on olla rauhainen.
Ei sinne yllä myrskysää sen korpikuuset piirittää
Ja aivan sattumalta sen löysin ruususen.(kert. loppuosa)

Kesäisen päivän helle vain häntä rakastaa,
ei itse tiedä raukka kelle hän kukoistaa.
Mutt' piikioksistansa kai hän villiruusun nimen sai.
Sä olet villiruusunen, ruusuista kaunehin.

Kesäisen sateen jälkeen kauneimmin kukoistaa,
oi minkä värivälkkeen tuo kukka silloin saa,
Mä silloin riennän luokse sen ja kukkiansa suutelen.
Sä olet villiruusunen, ruusuista kaunehin.

On ruusun kukat kauniit, niitt' en mä poimi pois
jos toiset ruusun vievät, se surun mulle tois.
Mä unhoittaisin kaiken muun, jos omakseni saisin sun,
Sä olet villiruusunen, ruusuista kaunehin.

Music sheet for Sing-Along and cast list for the comedy "Kosimassa" ("The Proposal"), presented at Kevättempaus-70

Social Events

On March 10, 1926, less than two months after Kansallisseura was formed, the club had its *alkajaisjuhla* (opening ceremony), a gala event that showcased the many and varied talents of the members. This was only the beginning—the first of several decades of social events that would follow.

In those days there was, of course, no television, no Finnish-language movies, and no professional forms of entertainment for Finns in Port Arthur. Also the supply of Finnish books and other publications was not extensive, and probably hard to come by. Thus the Finns in Port Arthur were hungry for any form of

Kansallisseura members in front of Orange Hall, possibly after the February, 1952 annual meeting: back row including: Mr. Erkki Kuokkanen, Mr. Jussi Niemelä, Mrs. Vera Jacobson and Mr. Niilo Viitala; middle row including: Mrs. Ellen Poutanen, Mrs. Vieno Rita and Mr. Aarne Rita; front row including: Mrs. Irene Suline and Mr. Väinö Jacobson (Photo from Kansallisseura archives)

entertainment in Finnish. To satisfy this demand, the various Finnish clubs stepped in. Kansallisseura members were nothing if not creative in their attempts to think up ways to fill the void and, at the same time, make money for the organization.

What follows is an attempt to compress the hundreds of social events that were put on during the three-quarters of a century of the club's existence, and to show the enthusiasm, creativity and hours of hard work involved.

Juhannus (Midsummer)

For Finns, Midsummer means countryside and lakes, and so already in the first summer, Kansallisseura held a *Juhannusjuhla* (Midsummer celebration) in Nolalu, with music by Sparks Orchestra. However, lacking private transportation in the early days, it must have been difficult to bring the paying public to the countryside. So in the years following, Kansallisseura members instead often gathered to celebrate Midsummer at a cottage for a picnic or a family day.

When, in 1951, Mr. Koivukoski offered his cottage for a Midsummer dance open to the public, Kansallisseura had to provide transportation for people without cars. The trucks left from 77 Secord Street at 6 p.m. The following is an account in the June 27 issue of *Canadan Uutiset* by an enthusiastic participant:

Group of Kansallisseura members at Koivukoski's cottage in 1945 (Photo from Kansallisseura archives)

Description of Juhannus, 1951 at Koivukoski's cottage from Canadan Uutiset

"So we had a real old-fashioned country shindig. There were tasty salads, sandwiches, coffee and even ice cream, prepared by the busy hard-working hostesses. And to top it off, the sauna was hot. One could bathe and swim. And a spectacular bonfire glowed on the surface of the lake, reminding us of our cherished childhood and the beautiful evenings of our youth, as we sang of the beloved shores, taking our yearning thoughts far beyond the ocean. And thus passed the evening, singing and enjoying the refreshments, and dancing to the music of an accordion."

Statement of Expenses and Receipts for the first Juhannus dance held at Surprise Lake camp on June 21, 1958. Reipas received $50.11 and Kansallisseura got $75.44 for their efforts.

Erkki Sirén on the shore of Surprise Lake early on a Juhannus morning in the 1970s (From the collection of Erkki Sirén)

With the purchase of the Surprise Lake camp, Kansallisseura now had a venue for holding Midsummer dances beside a lake "in the bosom of nature". The first of these was held in 1958 with Athletic Club Reipas.

"Expenses:
Admission ribbon	$1.50
CU Advertising	4.50
Orchestra	20.00
Prizes	8.50
Dartboard	5.18
	$39.68

Restaurant Expenses:
Food	$32.63
Kivelä	3.59
Milk	5.78
	42.00
Restaurant income	67.33
Restaurant expenses	42.00
Restaurant profit	$25.33

Receipts:
Admissions	$97.60
Sandbag throw	13.85
Darts	24.45
Sauna	4.00
	139.90
Expenses	39.68
	$100.22

Half donated to the Reipas team

Kansallisseura's share	$50.11
Restaurant profit	25.33
Total Profit	$75.44"

It is interesting to note that at this first *Juhannus* dance, the orchestra was paid $20.00, whereas at the last dance in 1996, the payment for the music had increased to $200.00.

For the next 38 years the camp provided a beautiful location for this traditional Finnish celebration. In the later years people sometimes stayed overnight in their vans, campers and trailers.

Lively music, traditional Finnish food and great dancing could always be counted upon. The raising of the Finnish and Canadian flags was another time-honoured tradition. But the *Juhannus kokko* (bonfire) sometimes was absent, because of dry conditions.

And then there were years when the lingering smoke from the dying bonfire and the gossamer morning mist floated over the calm lake in the first rays of the *Juhannus* sun. Could Finland offer anything lovelier!

Social Evenings

Today Finnish clubs usually hold their social events on a Saturday night, and only on major occasions like May Day, New Year or Midsummer. In the past entertainment was available almost every night of the week by one Finnish club or another. In order to entice the paying public to attend its events, a club had to be creative in what it offered. Kansallisseura members were especially talented

Flags flying over Surprise Lake camp at Midsummer (From the collection of Erkki Sirén)

in dreaming up various themes for their dances and social evenings.

Campers parked overnight at Surprise Lake camp during Midsummer in the 1970s (From the collection of Erkki Sirén)

The following is only a sampling of the kind of entertainment offered. Some of the events may be difficult to visualize by today's reader, but they were obviously familiar to the audience of the day. For example, everyone understood what a "Flower dance" was, whereas the "Sing Song evening" was a new concept, and was explained in detail in the newspaper article.

Could these Kansallisseura ladies be going to a Flower dance? Front row from left: Mrs. Edit Saasto, unidentified, Mrs. Vera Jacobson, two unidentified; Back row; Mrs. Toini Jacobson, Mrs. Helmi Tolvanen, Gloria Suline, unidentified, Mrs. Ellen Poutanen (Photo from Kansallisseura archives)

September, 1926: *Äijämiesten iltamat* (Married Men's dance) – with an unusually large organizing committee of thirteen men

May, 1928: *Liikkuvia kuvia Suomesta* (Moving pictures from Finland) – Music was played during the film, but the picture quality was poor and the text was badly translated into Finnish.

April, 1930: Social evening with solos by mezzo-soprano Miss Carin Wihlman, "straight from Paris", with Eli Kivinen playing on the *kantele*

May, 1930: Carnival dance

February, 1932: *Karkausiltamat* (Leap Year dance) – Women could ask men to dance and this made the event the most popular in ages.

November, 1933: Lottery evening with prizes, such as scissors, silk scarf for men, dress, cord of wood, skis and a violin

November, 1933: Family evening with impromptu performances, but the performers all turned out to be the same people as usual

March, 1934: Social evening, with *naputustanssi* (tap dancing) by Fred Sutton

May, 1934: Social evening organized by men, with a surprise speaker

August, 1934: *Kukkailtamat* (Flower dance) – It sounds lovely, but what was it?

December, 1937: At the 20th Independence Day celebration "little Finnish girl Eleanor Rae...amazed and delighted the audience with her gymnastic dancing." This very popular young lady continued to "amaze and delight" her audience for years, later performing exotic dances with her husband. Her numerous and elaborate costumes were always commented on in the press.

October, 1943: Social evening with Mrs. Fanny M. Heino from Sudbury as guest speaker. She spoke for over an hour and enthralled the audience, who wanted her back. She returned in November, 1945 and spoke for almost two hours.

November, 1943: *Vanhanmaantanssit* (Old Homeland dance)

January, 1944: Masquerade dance – People who dressed up were admitted free. Prizes were won by Mrs. Edit Koivukoski, Mrs. Aili Lahti and Mrs. Tyyne Aho.

April, 1944: Patriotic evening with a solemn and distinguished program to remind the audience of the suffering of the Finnish people during the war

May, 1944: Humorous entertainment by women

May, 1944: Free dance thanking people for their support of the Finnish war effort, sponsored by Mr. Leonard Kallio

March, 1945: *Merkkitanssit* (Spot dance)

May, 1945: May Day dance

March, 1946: Children's evening – Children ages 4 to 15 performed. Repeated later

March, 1946: *Huononajantanssit* (Hard Times dance) with a prize for the person dressed most shabbily

April, 1946: *Kori-iltamat* (Box social) – Women who had prepared a *"basketi jotain tavaraa"* (basket of some stuff) got in free and men bid on them. Evening also had *Onnentanssi* (Lucky dance, perhaps a spot dance).

November, 1946: Halloween dance – Profits went to buy shoes for children.

February, 1947: *Onkimailtamat* (Fishing social) – Fishing for prizes such as butter and sugar

April, 1947: Old Maids' and Widows' dance

May, 1947: *Palkintotanssit* (Prize dance) – Mrs. Järvelä donated *"nisu-ukon ja sima"* (doughboy and mead).

January, 1948: *Loppiaistanssit* (Twelfth Night dance)

March, 1948: *Windsorin Iloiset Rouvat* (The Merry Wives of Windsor) – Women organized a fun evening, including a funny poem, a mouth organ recital and three films, two of them about cancer. The event attracted a full house.

May, 1948: *Pumpulitanssit* (Gingham dance) – Obviously not a winner because they lost $5.12.

May, 1950: *Heimojuhlat* (Clan celebration with Estonians) - Both Otava and Estonian choirs performed. (Otava Choir was probably still a mixed choir at this time.)

June, 1950: *Paanatanssit* (Barn dance) – People dressed as if they were going haying

March, 1951: Coffee and dance evening for new immigrants - Prizes of $10.00, $15.00 and $25.00 were given out.

June, 1951: *Perhejuhla* (Family evening) – New immigrants were asked to perform. Otava Choir sang as a male choir.

December, 1952: *Tapanintanssit* (Boxing Day dance)

May, 1955: Lecture by Mr. Volu Varpio from Sudbury

December, 1955: *Kekritanssit* (All Saint's Day dance) - In December? Possibly an evening of feasting

July, 1959: Movie and coffee evening

September, 1962: *Venetsia ilta* (Evening in Venice)

Late 1960s: *Kevättempaus* (Spring Fling) – Pentti Junni, Eeva Sora and Maino Mannila sang *"Kallavesj"*, a song about a lake in the Savo province, while fishing from a tub of water. At the end, to the delight of the audience, they pulled out live fish.

August, 1972: *Kuutamotanssit* (Moonlight dance)

January, 1984: *Kaiken Kansan Humppatanssit* (Two-step dance for everyone) – Old time music, popular in the 1980s

January, 1987: Ami Vänskä with his orchestra visited from Finland.

June, 1990: Concert by baritone Kalle Kinnunen from Jyväskylä, Finland

One of the most popular events ever put on by Kansallisseura was the February 22, 1948 visit from Finland by Mr. J.O. Ikola, who told humorous stories in Ostrobothnian dialect as the character Vaasan Jaakkoo. People had been eagerly waiting for Mr. Ikola's performance, and came in such numbers *"...ettei 'pappi itte tahtonu kirkkohon sisälle päästä' ja että parisataa ihmistä jäi ulkopuolelle. Ylen juhlavan illan olivat järjestänehet, naiset silkis ja juhlapuvuus, suuri kuoro, monia soolo - ja duettoesityksiä. Kuoro kajahutti ensimmääseksi Sillanpään Marssilaulun ja monia muita isänmaallisia säveliä, joita kolmeen vuoteen en ollu Suomes enää kuullu."*[1] (...that 'even the minister almost didn't fit into the church', and that a

J.O. Ikola, as Vaasan Jaakkoo, boarding a train in Vaasa at the start of his 9-month North American tour.[2]

couple of hundred people had to stay outside. A very festive evening had been arranged, the women in silk and party dresses, large choir, many solo and duet performances. First the choir let ring out "Marching Song" by Sillanpää, and many other patriotic pieces, which I hadn't heard in Finland for three years.) Vaasan Jaakkoo stories are still enjoyed today by audiences especially at Ostrobothnian events.

These dances and social evenings were held at a variety of locations. In the beginning the Sons of England Hall, Italian Hall, Wallace Hall, and the Croatian Hall were used. Later Finlandia Club, Western Bearcat Hall, and Orange Hall became favourites, with Fort William Country Club as the chosen venue for some events.

Over the years many orchestras provided music for the dances: Kauko Kiviluoma Orchestra, H. Ekroos Orchestra, Helmi Hellen Orchestra, Jean McMichael Orchestra, Huugo & Kumppanit, Topi Jousmäen Trio, Armas Laakso Orchestra, Lyyski & Kumppanit, Kiven Orchestra, Pauli Arvo & Kumppanit, Vic Blazina Orchestra, Pelimannit, Souvaripojat, Serenaders, Al Jason's Melody Ranch Boys, and Elmer Rossi Orchestra.

It is interesting to observe how the number of social events listed earlier, gleaned from the available Kansallisseura records and *Canadan Uutiset,* reflect the changing conditions of the times. There was a large peak in immigration from Finland between 1923 and 1930. In the 1930s the number of club social events each year averaged around 12, with a high of 21 in 1930. This suggested that Kansallisseura provided a vital service to the Finnish population, many of whom were isolated by their language from the English-speaking community. Depression limited the funds available for entertainment, but the 25¢ price of admission to Kansallisseura events made them accessible.

Pentti, Topi and Matti playing rousing music for the dancers at Juhannus, 1979 (From the collection of Pentti Junni)

In the 1940s the war effort provided the incentive for the club to hold an average of 10 events each year, with a high of 15 in 1946. At this time fundraising for the Finnish war effort was the main goal.

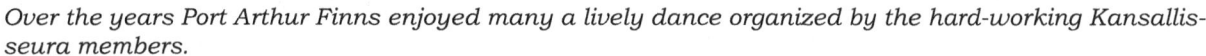

Over the years Port Arthur Finns enjoyed many a lively dance organized by the hard-working Kansallisseura members.

For the rest of Kansallisseura's history, the number of social events decreased dramatically to fewer than 5 per year. The fascination of television certainly kept audiences home, and building and maintaining the Surprise Lake camp shifted the focus from performance evenings to the Surprise Lake swim, picnics and ski meets, which now provided a different type of entertainment.

Theatre

In the beginning the social evenings sometimes consisted of a theatre performance, along with the usual musical numbers, poetry and speeches. Unfortunately no record was found of the names of these dedicated thespians, but the list of plays they put on is impressive. After the performance of "*Suuntalan häät*" ("The Wedding at Suuntala") on October 10, 1929, the earnest wish was expressed that plays should become a regular part of the social evenings, showing that they were popular with audiences. And so the year continued with three other plays:

"*Torpan Tyttö*" ("Crofter's Daughter")
"*Väinämöinen Tuonelassa*" ("Väinämöinen in Tuonela")
"*Harha-askeleita*" ("Gone astray")

In 1930 four productions were performed:
"*Mestarin nuuskarasia*" ("Master's Snuffbox")
"*Valkoinen Sankari*" ("The White Hero")
"*Päivärannan Onnelliset*" ("Happy Ones of Päiväranta")
"*Sininen kukkia*" (sic) ("The Blue Flower")

In 1931 there also were four plays:
"*Lehtoset ja Mehtoset*" ("Lehtonens and Mehtonens")
"*Torpantyttö*" (reprise)
"*Kattilan Talo*" ("The House of Kattila")
"*Kiusallinen palvelija*" ("Mischievous Servant")

In 1932 three plays were performed:
"*Taikayö*" ("Magic Night")
"*Kylänkellot*" ("Village Bells")
"*Porrassalmella*" ("At Porrassalmi")

In 1933 the audience was treated to:
"*Herrastapoja oppimassa*" ("Learning High Society Manners")
"*Pium Paun*"
"*Kihlaus*" ("Engagement")
"*Rakkauden vuoksi*" ("Because of Love")

In 1934 the six-year run of plays ended with the production of:
"*Isän haudalla*" ("At Father's Grave")
"*Elämän laulu*" ("Song of Life")

In 1944 there was yet another reprise of "*Torpan Tyttö*", a real favourite with audiences, perhaps because of its sentimental, melancholy theme. There were references to a "*melodraama*" in 1947. In a program from 1950, there was a "*tanssi kuvaelma lauluineen*" (short play with dancing and singing) as well as a melodrama.

Program for a social evening from November 2, 1950[3]

"The program is as follows:

Opening words – Irene Suline
Singing – 'You Are Our Dearest Land'
Accordion solo – Helvi Helle
Solo – Ellen Erkkilä
Poem – Kirsti Senick
Piano solo – Asta Layden
Duet – Hanna and Helmi
Speech – Kosti Koivukoski
Solo – Vera Jacobson
Melodrama – Helmi and Väinö, accompanied by Onni
Reading – Hilja Mannila
Solo – Helmi Tolvanen
Poem – Milja Järvinen
Something – Sulo Mannila
Short play with dancing and singing, accompanied by Helen Helle and Verna Richmond
Dancing at the end
Good orchestra   Admission 50¢"

According to Pentti Junni, in the later years Kansallisseura did sometimes put on short musicals, such as the one-act comedy, *"Kosimassa"* ("The Proposal") with the following cast:

Maiju, the farmer's daughter – Anja Nenonen
Mari, the maid – Eeva Mäkelä
Jaakko, the farmer – Pentti Junni
Aapeli – Arto Elonen
Santeri, the marriage broker – Osmo Mäkeläinen

"Ei Ikinä" ("No Way, Never!") was performed in 1970 with:

Anselmi – Arto Elonen
Hilma, his wife – Marjatta Lähteenmäki
Elvi, their daughter – Anja Hankila
Rauno, her fiancé – Tarmo Pihlaja
Kalle, a student – Osmo Mäkeläinen

Two other rather unusual forms of theatre were *varjokuvaelma* (shadow play) and *"tinamareski."* The latter comes from the French word *tintamarresque*, a type of harlequin theatre, where the background and the body of a person are painted on a board that is between the audience and the actors. In place of faces there are holes through which the actors put their heads. Today *tintamarresque* is used mainly for humorous photographs.

Modern example of tintamarresque *(From the collection of Raili Garth)*

Pikkujoulut (Christmas parties)

Kansallisseura Christmas parties were the most regularly held event. The first one was in 1926 at Wallace Hall and except for a few years in the late 1930s, served as an annual get-together until 1998. The parties were usually free and the activity was directed towards children in those years when the members had young families.

During the Depression Kansallisseura made an extra effort to accommodate the single Finnish men who worked at the government road camps around Port Arthur, by organizing a Christmas party for them on December 24, 1931. An undated newspaper clipping found in the Kansallisseura files describes the event.

"Extra trains brought hundreds of men to town for Christmas from the government road camps to celebrate with their relatives, whoever had them. Most of those who did not have families stayed at the camp, except the Finnish men of this area who have many friends in town. Kansallisseura organized especially for these men without homes a Christmas party on Christmas Eve, and there sure were a lot of people present. The tree was beautifully decorated, the program was warm and created a homey feeling, and even lots of gifts were exchanged. And after that, when hefty portions of rice pudding were eaten and cups of hot coffee were consumed with a variety of breads, boy, did the evening itself begin to taste like a celebration for everyone."

Article describing a Christmas party held by Port Arthur Kansallisseura for single men from the road camps in 1931

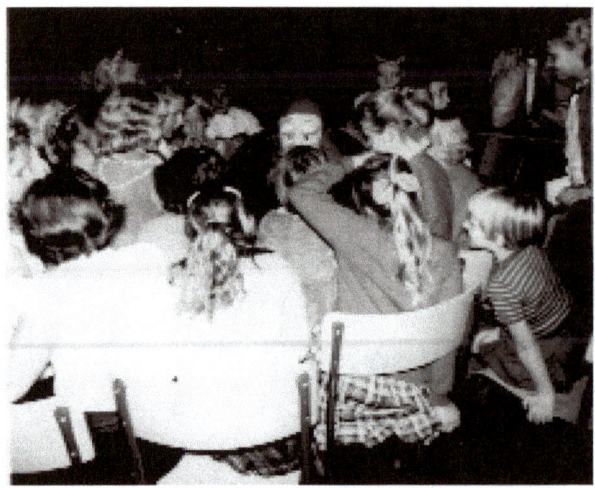

A rather scary Joulupukki surrounded by children at a Kansallisseura Christmas party in 1959 (From the collection of Kaarina Brooks)

Santa unmasked! Toini Jacobson is surprised to discover that Joulupukki is actually Veikko Parviainen (From the collection of K. Brooks)

Quartet performing at a Nor-Shor Club Christmas party circa 1960. From left: Teuvo Sorvisto, Reino Erkkilä, Olavi Laine, Pentti Junni and Pekka Kuisma with his accordion. Listening on the right are Toini Parviainen, Väinö Jacobson and Hanna Mannila. (From the collection of Pentti Junni)

Children performing "Tonttujen Jouluyö" ("Christmas Night of the Elves") at Kansallisseura Christmas party in 1968. (From the collection of Pentti Junni)

In the early years, Kansallisseura provided the coffee and Christmas pudding, as well as candy for the children. As times changed, parents were asked to bring a gift. These Christmas parties were so popular that the *Pikkujoulu* in 1966 attracted 50 children. For about the last 25 years, Kansallisseura held the Christmas parties in conjunction with other Finnish clubs in Thunder Bay.

---

[1] Ikola, J.O., *Vaasan Jaakkoo rapakon takana 1947-48,* (Helsinki: Werner Söderström Osakeyhtiö, 1949) p. 345.
[2] Ibid., p. 15.
[3] *Canadan Uutiset*, November 1, 1950.

Charitable Work

Right from the beginning, Port Arthur Kansallisseura was active in raising the material standards of the local Finnish people. For example, only a month after its founding, members discussed setting up a restaurant and a rooming house to assist the young men, who had arrived in Port Arthur during the immigration peaks of 1923 and 1924. While this generous proposal was never actualized, the club did join in April with the church and a youth group to hold a social evening, with the proceeds directed towards helping Mr. Jaakko Korpi. This shows that even at the beginning, when its finances were very precarious, Kansallisseura had its heart in the right place.

Since sports were such an important part of the Finnish community, Kansallisseura participated in Olympic Fundraising, starting with the Amsterdam Games in 1928. In 1932 dances were held to assist the Finnish Olympians going to Los Angeles. By this time the Central Organization of Loyal Finns in Canada (COLFC) had made the Olympic Games part of its fundraising, so the money collected by Port Arthur was combined with that from other branches.

In 1952 the Olympic Games were held in Finland and to support the Finnish team, Kansallisseura organized a fundraising concert at the Paramount Theatre in Port Arthur. Among the performers for the evening were Toini and Väinö Jacobson, Arthur Kajander, Norma Ristimäki, Eva and Matti Romu, Raymond and Vaima Myllari, and Sulo Kari.

The donations received during the annual Finnish Independence Day celebrations were usually directed towards *Suomen yhdistyneille koteja kodittomille lapsille* (Homes for the Homeless Children) in Finland. This generated thousands of Finn markkas over the many years that the event was held under the auspices of Kansallisseura.

The Depression in the 1930's was, of course, a serious challenge for many Finns in the Port Arthur area, and here again Kansallisseura came to the aid of its members. Fortunately by this time the resources of the club were such that they were in a better position to help. At the executive meeting on October 2, 1930, Mr. Kosti Koivukoski proposed "...that since a very hard winter is expected, and since many of our men will be unemployed, we should solicit, and also if we don't receive enough, should buy with the club's funds, foodstuff, from which the women of the club could then prepare meals for our men in need." The motion was carried.

The following year, at a monthly meeting held at K. Euren farm in Intola on June 7, it was decided to extend loans to those members who were in financial difficulties. This was done, and by the end of 1932 all the loans had been repaid. During the year Mr. Ketonen gave potatoes from his farm to Kansallisseura members to supplement their diet.

Finnish Aid Society

On November 25, 1939 Mr. Kosti Koivukoski, the deputy consul of Finland, chaired a meeting at the Sons of England Hall in Port Arthur. Its purpose was to establish *Thunder Bayn piirin Suomalainen Punainen Risti* (Thunder Bay District Finnish Red Cross) and he assumed the role of the chairman in this new organization for the next few years. In the beginning, for the first eight years, the organization operated under the name of *Suomen Avustusyhdistys* (The Finnish Aid Society), after which it converted back to its original name.[1] Membership in the Aid Society was made up of people from every Finnish organization in Port Arthur, except those on the Left of the political spectrum. Kansallisseura members were key participants in this endeavour, enthusiastically contributing their time and energy.

It is important not to confuse the Finnish Aid Society with the *Canadan Suomiapu* (Canada-Finland Aid Society Fund) that was active in Toronto after the war in 1946. The former was comprised of people living in and around Port Arthur and excluded the Left. The latter included all Finnish Canadians from coast to coast, regardless of political affiliation, as discussed in more detail later under "Kansallisseura War Effort" on page 72.

The Winter War had ended on March 13, 1940, and now it was possible to send money and parcels to help the people back home. Thus most of the Finnish social life in Port Arthur, starting in 1940, revolved around the activities set up by the Finnish Aid Society. For example, the week of March 24 was designated as Finnish Week, and a different event was held every night to raise funds for Finland. Almost the only non-Society events were the weekly dances and the monthly plays that were performed at *Työn Temppeli* (Labour Temple).

The Finnish Aid Society sold $1.00 memberships very aggressively and was able to recruit over 500 members in its first year. It had *vaatekomitea* (clothing committee), *huvitoimikunta* (entertainment committee), and *kerhohuonetoimikunta* (meeting room committee). An official flag, made by the women's committee, was presented in June of 1940 to the executive with great ceremony.

The pace of fundraising activity in the first year was furious, but *Canadan Uutiset* reported in its November 6, 1940 issue that people seemed to be getting tired of attending all the events. The article exhorted them to come and keep supporting the charity. By February of 1941 the Aid Society had sent an impressive total of $19,925.00 to Finland. Also on February 14, 1941 it opened up *Suomi Tupa* on Secord Street in the old Ladigan Pharmacy building, which became the centre of the club's activities. Coffee was served all day, and on opening day they collected $38.60, which was more than a month's rent. The rooms were also used for meetings and social events. However, the activity never reached the initial enthusiasm, and in 1941 membership in the Society dropped to 83.

Then on June 30, 1941 Finland was again at war with Russia, and aid could no longer reach the people. This *Jatkosota* (Continuation War) was different, in that Russia had now joined the Allies. Thus the Finns in Canada were required to register as "enemy aliens", although this was never enforced. To show their loyalty to their new homeland, the Aid Society now began to hold events to raise money for the Canadian Red Cross and British orphans. The largest of these fundraisers, held on February 13, 1942 with Canadian and Finnish performers, was attended by 800 people and netted $204.35 for the Canadian Red Cross. Some of the money was also used to buy Victory Bonds to support the Allied cause.

The annual meeting of the Aid Society on February 25 was reported by *Canadan Uutiset* on March 4, 1942.

Report in Canadan Uutiset *on the February 18, 1942 meeting of Finnish Aid Society*

"At the meeting the question of the society's continuation was brought up. After discussion and voting, the meeting decided, with a large majority, to continue the work of the association. It was suggested that now, during the war, more attention should be paid to assisting Canada and England.

Executive for the next year was elected as: Chairman - Mr. Chas. Stenback, Treasurer - Mr. Hans Saasto and other executive members: Mr. Emil Mäki, Mr. J. Rönkkö, Mr. Puustinen, Mr. Lauri Korolainen, Mrs. Albrecht, Mrs. L. Faure, Mrs. Ranta and in reserve Mrs. Vera Jacobson, Mrs. H. Wälmä and Mrs. F. Salo."

The events held by the Finnish Aid Society were similar to the ones organized by Kansallisseura in the past: masquerade dances, social evenings with a program and plays, coffee dances, Kalevala celebrations in 1943, etc. It is likely that by 1942 many of the Kansallisseura members, who had participated in the activities, had returned back to the revitalized Kansallisseura.

The last event held at *Suomi Tupa* was on January 27, 1946, after which the meetings were held at *Työn Temppeli*. At the beginning of 1948 the name of the Aid Society was changed back to the original, Thunder Bay District Finnish Red Cross. The organization was still holding social evenings at the end of 1951, and ceased to function around 1960.

Kansallisseura War Effort

When Kansallisseura was revived in 1942, it set out with new enthusiasm to collect funds for sending to Finland after peace would be restored, since no money or parcels could be sent during the war. The financial journals from 1942 to 1945 provide interesting details of the club's efforts to accumulate the sum of $500.00. What follows is a detailed description of how, penny by penny, dance by dance, Port Arthur Kansallisseura slowly accumulated the funds over four years. When one considers that a cup of coffee brought in 15¢ and a bottle of pop 7¢, one can see why it took so long.

Following are the details for a social evening, that was held on May 30th, 1944 and generated a profit of $14.06. It shows how hard the *Huvitoimikunta* (Entertainment Committee) worked, and how they gave a reckoning for every penny earned and spent.

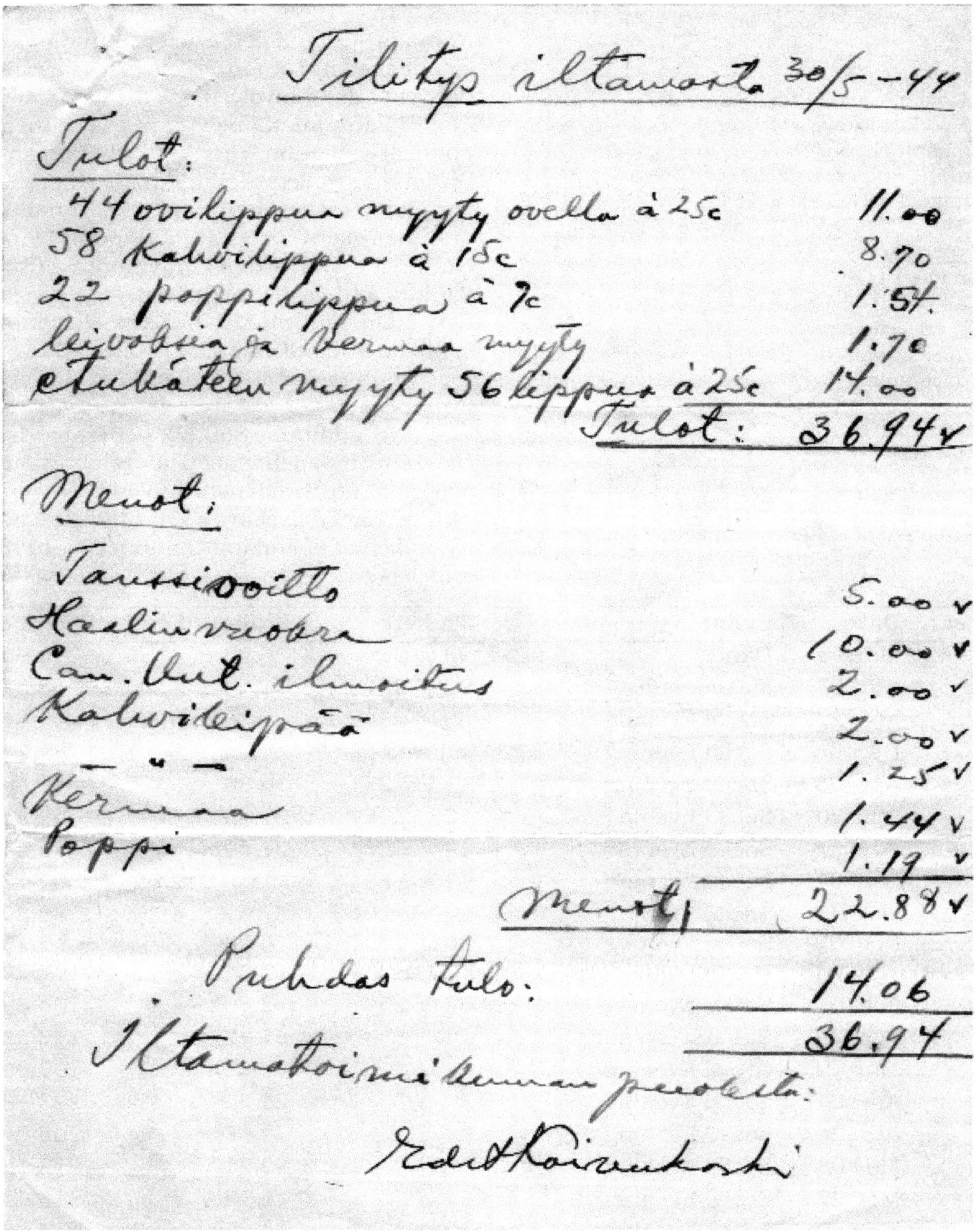

Tilitys iltamasta 30/5 -44

Tulot:
- 44 ovilippua myyty ovella à 25c — 11.00
- 58 kahvilippua à 15c — 8.70
- 22 poppilippua à 7c — 1.54
- leivoksia ja kermaa myyty — 1.70
- etukäteen myyty 56 lippua à 25c — 14.00

Tulot: 36.94

Menot:
- Tanssivoitto — 5.00
- Haalin vuokra — 10.00
- Can. Uut. ilmoitus — 2.00
- Kahvileipää — 2.00
- — " — — 1.25
- Kermaa — 1.44
- Poppi — 1.19

Menot: 22.88

Puhdas tulo: 14.06

36.94

Iltamatoimikunnan puolesta:

Edit Koivukoski

Statement of Income and Expenses for the May 30, 1944 social evening that netted the club $14.06

"Accounting of Social on 30/5 - 44

Income:
44 tickets sold at the door @ 25¢	11.00
58 coffee tickets @15¢	8.70
22 pop tickets @ 7¢	1.54
Baking and cream sold	1.70
Pre-sold 56 tickets @ 25¢	14.00
Income	36.94

Expenses:
Orchestra	5.00
Hall rental	10.00
CU advertising	2.00
Coffee bread	2.00
Coffee bread	1.25
Cream	1.44
Pop	1.19
Expenses	22.88
Profit	14.06
	36.94

On behalf of the entertainment committee:
Edit Koivukoski"

In 1946 *Canadan Suomiapu* (Canada-Finland Aid Society Fund) was established in Toronto. "This drive in support of Finland involved, for the first time, all Finnish Canadians regardless of their political affiliation."[2] By 1947 this organization had collected $76,037.65 from the various member clubs across Canada, and had sent over 20,000 pounds of clothing, shoes, penicillin, vitamins, first aid kits and yarns to Finland.

On May 4, 1946 Kansallisseura sent the $500.00 they had collected over four years to Canada-Finland Aid Society Fund.

In addition, $63.59, generated by the 1945 Independence Day celebration, was sent to Sweden to aid Finnish orphans. Kansallisseura's charitable activity on behalf of Finland continued in 1946 and 1947.

Year	Date	Event	Tickets	Profit	Loss	Balance
1942	Mar. 18	Dance	93 @ 25¢	6.93		6.93
	Apr. 08	Masquerade	92 @ 25¢	1.64		8.57
	Apr. 22	Social Evening	80 @ 25¢		0.76	7.81
	Dec. 06	Social Evening	collection	17.26		**25.07**
1943	Apr. 06	Social Evening	115 @ 25¢	16.39		41.46
	Apr. 20	Social Evening	108 @ 25¢	21.39		62.85
	June 01	Social Evening	180 @ 25¢	27.59		90.44
	Sep. 07	Social Evening	115 @ 25¢		2.66	87.78
	Oct. 05	Social Evening	179 @ 25¢		1.39	86.39
	Nov. 02	Social Evening	89 @ 25¢	0.36		**86.75**
1944	Jan. 04	Masquerade	130 @ 25¢	17.54		104.29
	Feb. 01	Social Evening	86 @ 25¢	2.60		106.89
	Feb. 29	Cabaret Evening		85.42		192.31
	Mar. 21	Social Evening		7.65		199.96
	Apr. 04	Social Evening		23.54		223.50
	Apr. 24	Social Evening		39.47		262.97
	May 08	Social Evening		49.21		312.18
	May 22	Social Evening		6.22		318.40
	May 30	Social Evening	100 @ 25¢	14.06		**332.46**
1945	Apr. 03	Men's Social Evening	388 @ 25¢	105.18		437.64
	May	From *Huvitoimikunta*		67.87		505.51
	Oct. 02	Social Evening	101 @ 25¢	18.48		**523.99**

Details showing how Kansallisseura accumulated $500.00 over four years.

Receipt for $500.00 donation to Canada-Finland Aid Society Fund, collected from 1942 to 1945 by Port Arthur Kansallisseura

To show their loyalty to Canada during the war years, Kansallisseura also gave aid to Canadian charities. For example, in 1943 the following toys were purchased for $26.68:

"wrapping paper, string, stickers
1 Monopoly, 2 beauty sets
2 pairs of socks
2 powder puffs
1 table tennis
1 can of building sticks
1 Courando set
1 Fighting Force toy set
1 Canadian Fighters, 1 big doll
1 nurse kit, 2 small dolls
2 pairs of doll socks
1 army hat, 1 drum, 1 gun
1 wagon and blocks, 1 mop
1 floor sweeper, 1 broom
2 doll beds, 1 yoyo
1 box of crayons
1 colouring book
1 Up and Down game
1 children's jewelry, 1 brooch
2 purses, 2 combs
2 hair ribbons
1 horse and 1 drummer"

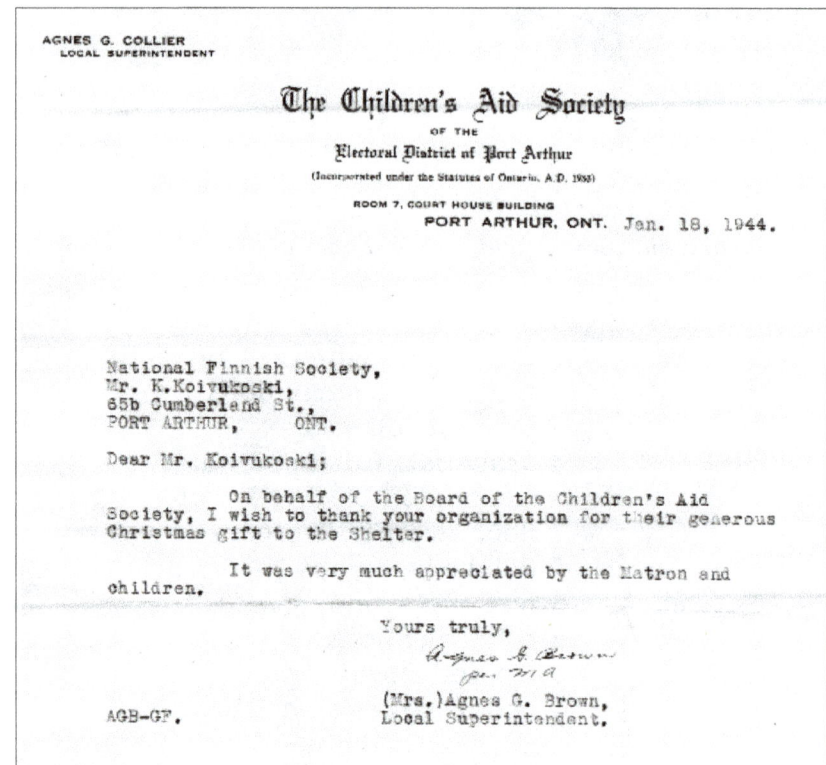

Toys sent to Canadian orphans in 1943 by Kansallisseura

Thank you note received for Christmas gifts sent to Canadian children by Kansallisseura

The toys were then sent to provide Christmas gifts to the children in the Children's Aid Society shelter. Kansallisseura received the thank you note on the left from Mrs. Agnes Brown, the Local Superintendent.

After the war, in 1946, when once again parcels could be sent to Finland, Kansallisseura women were busy buying and packing necessities. Each parcel could weigh no more than 15 pounds, and was addressed to a specific recipient in Finland, as shown in the example on the following page:

Lähettäjä Mrs W.M. Pakka
241 Ray Blvd.

3 kpl. Poikain housuja
4 paria puoli kenkiä
2 kpl kampaa
kummi nauhaa
silmi neuloja
parsi neuloja
1 villa pusero

2 p. Tyttöin housut
1 Tytön lōninki.
1 liivi hame ja pusero
1 lōninki kangas
4 Rullalankaa
1 lbs Kahvia

S. Kaskela
Raahe
Kiilakosken Posti 2.90

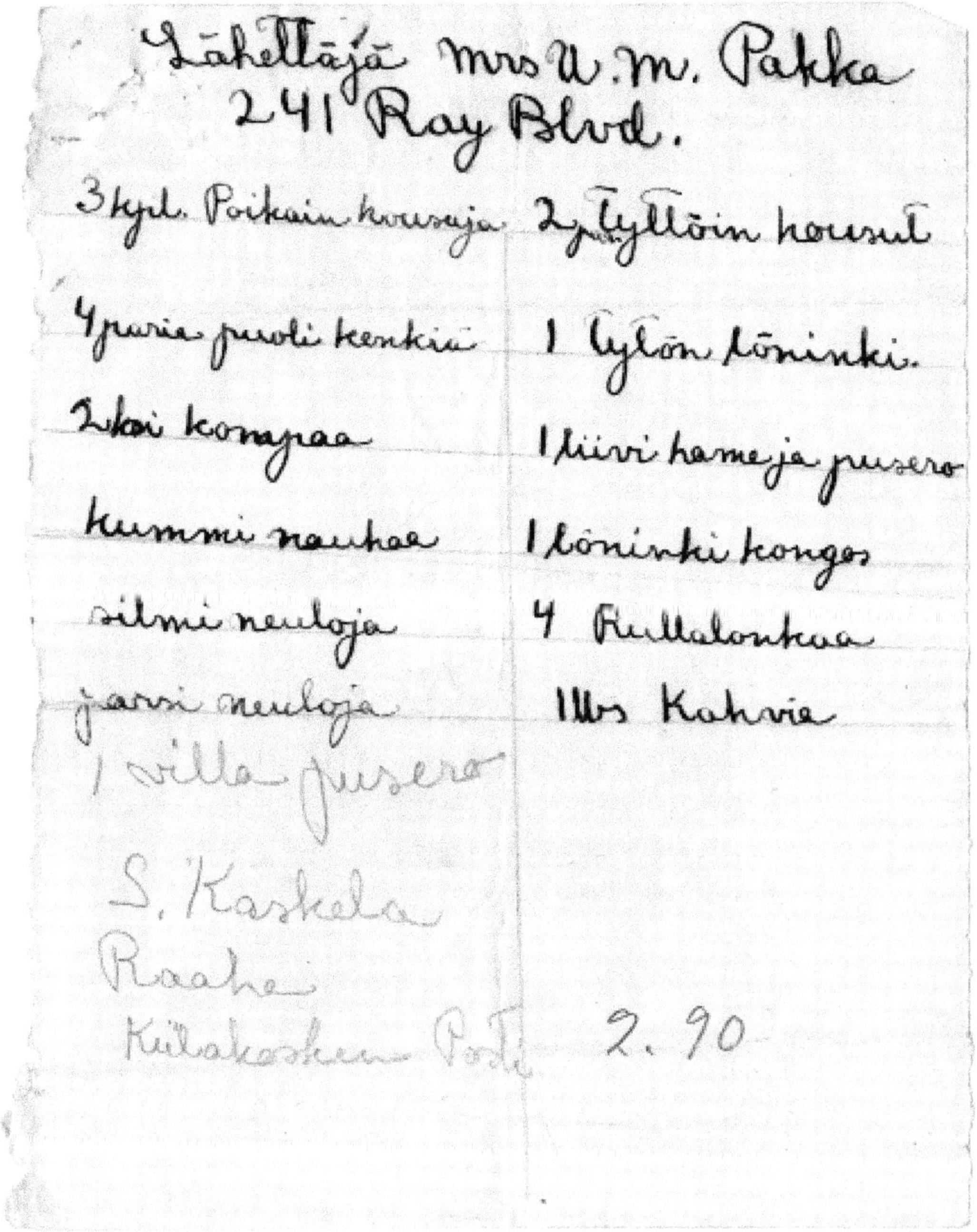

Items purchased for a parcel sent by Mrs. W.M. Pakka to S. Kaskela in Raahe, Finland

"Sender Mrs W.M. Pakka
241 Ray Blvd.

3 pairs of boy's pants
4 pairs of ankle shoes
2 combs, elastic
sewing needles
darning needles
1 woolen sweater
2 pairs of girl's pants

1 girl's dress
1 jumper and blouse
fabric for 1 dress
4 spools of thread
1 pound of coffee.

S.Kaskela
Raahe
Kiilakosken Posti 2.90."

A. K. GRAHAM, K.C.
PRESIDENT - TORONTO, ONT.

A. VUORINEN
EXECUTIVE SECRETARY

Canada-Finland Aid Society Fund
CANADAN SUOMIAPU

REGIST. No. C-4109

HEADQUARTERS: 307 STERLING TOWER BLDG., TORONTO 1, ONT.
DEPOT: 60 BEDFORD ROAD, TORONTO 5, ONT.

Elokuun 22, 1946

TRUSTEES:

GEORGE BAGWELL
HON. TREASURER - TORONTO

SVEN STADIUS,
PETER MERTANEN,
SECRETARIES - TORONTO

EMIL SALIN - TORONTO

H. ILOMAKI - TORONTO

BOARD OF DIRECTORS:

EINO UNHOLA - TORONTO
CHAIRMAN OF THE BOARD

AILI MALM - VANCOUVER
HELGE EKENGREN - VANCOUVER
TYYNE SILLMAN - PORT ARTHUR
C. A. STENBACK - PORT ARTHUR
W. EKLUND - SUDBURY
P. RUOHONEN - SUDBURY
V. LAHTI - COPPER CLIFF
I. MAKYNEN - TIMMINS
E. LAAKSO - TIMMINS
V. KIIVERI - TORONTO
G. SUNDQVIST - TORONTO
REV. J. YRTTIMAA - MONTREAL
N. RAJALA - MONTREAL

Mr. Väinö Jacobson,
212 Van Horne Str.,
Port Arthur, Ont.

Arv. Mr. Jacobson:

Port Arthurin Suomalaisen Kansallisseuran Mr. K. Koivukosken pyynnöstä lähetämme Teille oheellisena 10 kpl. Nuorten ensiapulaatikko-keräyslistaa, N:t 2063-2072 ja toivomme parasta menestystä toiminnallenne.

Suomesta on ilmoitettu että siellä tarvitaan tällaisia laatikoita kipeästi ja he voisivat niitä käyttää 3000 kappaletta, joten tietysti koetamme lähettää niin monta kuin mahdollista, vaikkapa emme voisikaan koko määrää täyttää. Laatikkojen hinta on $3.25 kappale suoraan tehtaasta toimitettuna.

Kunnioittaen,

CANADA-FINLAND AID SOCIETY FUND
CANADAN SUOMIAPU

per *[signature]*

Liitteenä: 10 keräyslistaa.

Letter dated August 22, 1946 from Canada-Finland Aid Society Fund asking Kansallisseura to collect money for first aid kits for schools

In 1946, $343.35 was sent for first aid kits to Finnish schools, and a further $464.59 was collected in 1947 from the various events held during the year.

"At the request of Mr. K. Koivukoski of the Port Arthur Kansallisseura we are sending you 10 fundraising lists, No. 2063-2072, for young people's first aid kits, and we wish the best success in your endeavour.

We have been notified by Finland that they sorely need these first aid kits and they could use 3000 of them. So of course we will try to send as many as possible, even if we cannot fill the whole order. The price is $3.25 per box, delivered straight from the factory."

One of the more unique and popular fundraisers in 1947 was *Korvikenäyttely* (Substitute Exhibition), which toured throughout USA and Canada. It was a collection of close to 200 objects that had been invented by Finns for use during the lean war years. The articles showed the ingenuity of the Finnish population in replacing unavailable materials with home-grown ones. Included were clothing, shoes, utensils, everyday articles, etc. For example, lacking leather, shoes were made with wooden soles and paper uppers.

> Näytteille oli tuotu kaikellaista korutavaraa, puuveistostöitä, tauluja, paperipöytäliinoja, pellavakudonnaisia, villakudonnaisia, pitsikudoksia ja olipa puukenkiä ja aamukenkiä paperista valmistettuja y.m. Kaikki työt olivat taidokkaasti valmistettuja ja kauniita nähdä, mutta käytössä tietenkin ne eivät ole kovin ensiluokkaisia. Vieläpä saatiin oikeata kahvikorviketta maistaa, ja nyt me vasta oikein käsitämme kuinka suuresta merkityksestä on Suomessa saada kahvipaketti jouluksi.

Article from undated Canadan Uutiset, *in March, 1947 describing the* Korvikenäyttely

"On display were various pieces of jewelry, wooden carvings, paintings, paper tablecloths, linen and wool textiles, crochet lace articles and there were even wooden shoes and slippers made from paper, etc. All the items were well crafted and beautiful to see, but in use they were, of course, not first class. We even had the opportunity to sample *kahvikorviketta* (coffee substitute) and now we can really understand what a great thing it is in Finland to receive a package with coffee for Christmas."

The two shipping containers, which weighed about 250 pounds, came to Port Arthur from Sudbury, and were sent on to Vancouver after the exhibition. When Kansallisseura put on the exhibit, almost 390 tickets were sold at 35¢ each, generating $230.00 for the Canada-Finland Aid Society Fund.

Fundraising in Later Years

By the end of the 1940s, the intensity of fundraising activities had cooled down considerably, but coffee parcels were still being sent to Finland in 1949 and even later. Bingo games as fundraisers were started in February of 1951 at the Italian Hall. Workers were given a free bottle of pop, and the funds collected were donated to Canadian Red Cross, the Finnish Independent Church, and others.

When there was an opportunity to do some major fundraising, Kansallisseura took advantage of it. For example, on August 7, 1952, Armi Kuusela, the reigning Miss Universe, made a stop in Port Arthur. The club arranged a ball, generating $644.60 that was donated to *Sotainvaliidiveljesliitto* (Brotherhood of War Invalids). Miss Kuusela received roses and a $10.00 gift of "*hieno porsliininen muistoesine*" (fancy porcelain souvenir). The event was held at the Current River Casino and was attended by almost 1000 people. Mr. Paavo Lehtonen handed Miss Kuusela an address containing 400 names of Finns in the area, with the following text:

"We wish to extend our congratulations to you, Miss Kuusela, on the occasion of having been crowned Miss Universe, and express our joy at the honour that, because of your beauty, has fallen upon our beloved homeland."[3]

In 1952, money was donated towards the statue of K.G.E. Mannerheim, collected by *Suomen Aseveljet-Amerikan*

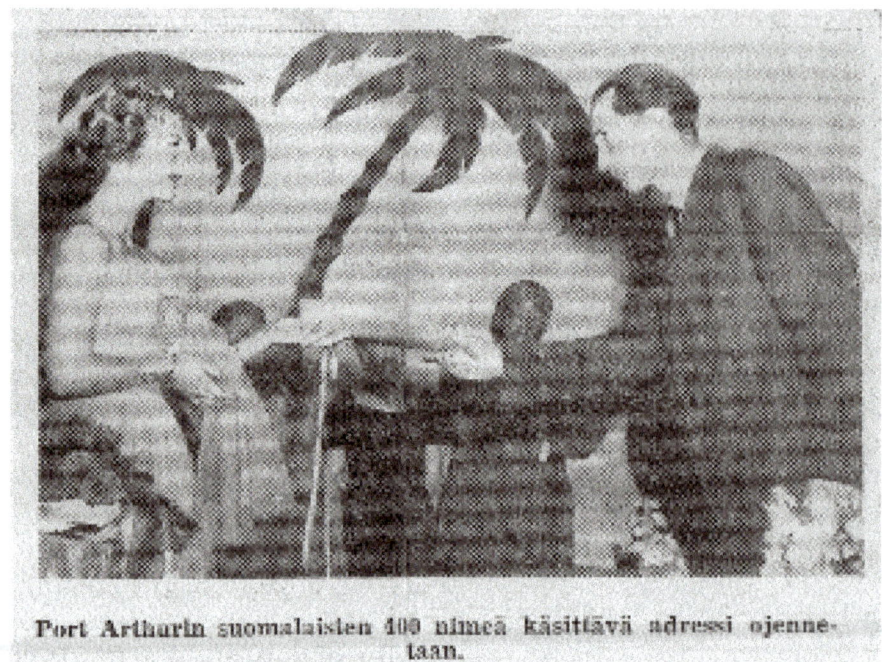

Paavo Lehtonen handing Miss Universe, 1952, Armi Kuusela an address containing the names of 400 Port Arthur Finns

yhdistys (Finnish Veterans in America) in New York. Independence Day celebrations and the resulting donations to Homes for the Homeless Children ended in 1953. And although, after 1955, most of Kansallisseura's funds went to the purchase and upkeep of the camp at Surprise Lake, the club still participated in some charitable activities each year. Over the years they made donations to the Finnish Language School, European Flood Relief, Canadian Cancer Society, exchange student fund,

Making a donation in 1964 to Dawson Court from Kansallisseura are Walter Wanson, John Niemelä, Acting Mayor Alderman Wilmont and Toini Jacobson (From the collection of Väinö Jacobson Jr.)

Reetta Junni standing beside the Finnish immigrant monument at the International Friendship Gardens in 1976 (From the collection of Pentti Junni)

Finn Time TV program, Thunder Bay Symphony, Rita Music Scholarship at Lakehead University, Finland's 75th Independence Day Committee, Canadian Suomi Foundation and Dawson Court Seniors' Home.

In the 1970s Kansallisseura participated in a project called the International Friendship Gardens, which was the Centennial project of the local Soroptimist Club. It involved several ethnic groups in Port Arthur, who each created a garden "symbolic of their homeland and its culture" on land donated by Fort William. For the first time since the 1940s, when they worked on the Finnish Aid Society, the Thunder Bay Finnish community joined forces to build a grand memorial to Finnish immigrants. Many Kansallisseura members worked on the site, with Pentti Junni taking on the role of the project leader. Kansallisseura also helped financially by donating funds in 1975, and providing a loan in 1980.

When the camp at Surprise Lake was sold, the club made further donations to the Finlandia Club Building Fund ($20,000.00), Hilldale Lutheran Church ($20,000.00), Thunder Bay Regional Hospital Foundation ($10,000.00), Finnish Male Singers of North America ($1,000.00), *Thunder Bayn Pelimannikerho* ($2,000.00) and Canadian Suomi Foundation ($1,000.00).

Kansallisseura did, indeed, have its heart in the right place.

---

[1] *Canadan Uutiset*, November 9, 1949.
[2] Lindstrom-Best, Varpu, "Central Organization of the Loyal Finns in Canada," *Polyphony: The Bulletin of the Multicultural History Society of Ontario, Finns in Ontario*, (Vol. 3, No. 2, Fall 1981) p. 103.
[3] *Canadan Uutiset*, July 17, 1952.

Sports

Port Arthur Kansallisseura considered sports an important part of its mandate, and was supportive of all endeavours that improved the physical well-being of its members.

Sports and Gymnastic Club Kiri

During the 1920s several good athletes, who had been district champions and had belonged to the Gymnastic and Sports Federation of Finland, immigrated to Canada. They were keen to start a similar organization in their new homeland and so, on April 24, 1930, supported by Kansallisseura, about twenty sports-minded people met at the Savo Cafe to discuss the possibility of starting an athletic club. Just two weeks later, on the 20th of April, this club had its first meeting. About 43 people were in attendance and Aarne Rita was chosen as the chairman. Eeli Niskala, Einari Auvola, Ville Kärkkäinen and Paavo Laitinen were the other members of the executive. This new Sports and Gymnastic Club was called Kiri.

A month later, the first competition was held on Victoria Day, May 24, at Shuniah Park, among the members of Kiri. Despite the cold weather, many spectators were present. One of the main events was the pentathlon, which included shot put, high jump, long jump and the triple jump—with and without a running start. Aarne Rita was the clear winner with 325.16 points; Kalle Autio was second with 316.35 points and Armas Karonen came third with 314.92 points. There was also a 1500 metre cross-country run, which Aarne Rita completed in 5:14, a very good time, considering the difficult terrain and the cold weather. Arvi Ristimäki was second with 5:41 and Väinö Kokko took the bronze with the time of 6 minutes even. Fourth place went to Kalle Autio who finished 21 seconds later. Women competed in a 100 metre sprint, won by Lilja Unkuri with a time of 15 seconds. Esteri Tikkanen came in a second later and Viola Latvala clocked in at 19 seconds.

Prizes were awarded that night at a social evening organized by Kiri, where Mr. K. Koivukoski delivered a speech on Finnish *sisu*. Mr. Wickström gave an artistic performance on the violin accompanied by Miss Sheare, and Mr. Jolkka recited a poem and sang a comic song. This first Kiri soirée ended with very lively dancing.[1]

Several other sporting events were organized by Kiri in 1930. The July 23 issue of *Canadan Uutiset* describes the first intercity event, held on July 19 against Fort William, where many district records were broken. The following excerpt is a colourful play-by-play description of the 5x1000 relay (shown on the left):

> "The most exciting test was perhaps the 5x1000 metre relay. Kiri had put five of its best stallions into the fire, namely K. Autio, A. Ristimäki, T. Niemi, V. Kokko and A. Rita, with the men running in the above order. Against them was the YMCA team from Fort William. When the boys took off and the first exchange neared, from the bleachers, filled mainly with male Kiri sports fans and female Kiri supporters, could be heard feminine melancholy sighs, when our first runner Autio was left behind by his Canadian competitor. At the exchange point the distance between the runners had stretched quite a bit, and our women were already wondering how the Kiri boys would fare. The male sports experts, however, did not become nervous because they knew that the Canadians had placed their fastest man first (except the 5th, who was even better, namely Swartz), thus probably planning to discourage the Finns right at the beginning, but they also knew that each Kiri man was better than the last, with Rita himself as the anchorman. When the second runner took off, the women let out a joyful screech because young Arvi Ristimäki sprang forward at a tremendous speed, carrying the baton he had received from Autio, running towards the waiting Niemi. Ristimäki ran fabulously well, in our estimation his best 1000 metres, but unfortunately his speed was not recorded. The distance between the runners began to shorten quickly and soon a powerful war cry rang out when Ristimäki, hair streaming behind him, ran past his competitor and arrived much before him to the second exchange. Niemi grabbed the baton and started off with lightning speed to take it forward, increasing by a considerable margin the spread Ristimäki had begun. And so it

continued, man by man. Kokko ran like a trooper without letting the spread shorten, and when Rita got the baton in his possession, the results were clear to us. Although Swartz tried his best, he saw at the end how things stood, and Rita cut the tape in fine form about 150 metres ahead of Swartz. A loud hurrah rang out for our gallant boys."

Another field day, organized for the members of Kiri, was held on September 7. The most exciting event that day was the tug-o-war between the old-timers and the young men, won by the latter team. Free coffee was served to the spectators. The prizes were presented at a dance on Sept.13, 1930.

Although most of the sporting events were held in the summer, in February and March of 1931 Kiri organized ski races, one of them on Lake Superior.

After about a year of operating within Kansallisseura, Kiri separated and began life as an independent sports club. The reason, given by Aarne Rita in a taped interview, was that Kansallisseura did not support Kiri in the acquisition of sporting equipment, such as javelins, shot puts, etc. In the interview Mr. Rita relates that the prizes were seldom "hardware"—medals or trophies. Instead the local businesses donated items such as a suitcase, a sack of potatoes, clothing, or a sack of sugar from the Kivelä bakery. Mr. Rita remembers winning a week's worth of meal coupons from Hoito Restaurant.[2]

No record of Kiri activities was found in *Canadan Uutiset* after 1932, but Mr. Rita maintains that Kiri was active for five or six years. In an article written on August 20, 1931, *Canadan Uutiset* stated that "*Kirin miehet ovat saavuttaneet mainetta paikallisten ennätysten rikkojina ja kohottaneet Kirin huomatuimmaksi seuraksi tässä osassa maata myös toiskielisten keskuudessa.*" (The men of Kiri have achieved fame by breaking local records, and have elevated Kiri to be the most prominent sports club in this part of the country, even among the English speakers.)

In its heyday the club had close to 80 members and many records were broken by its athletes. In the taped inverview Mr. Rita proudly relates that in 1929, under less than ideal conditions, he had run the mile in 4:23:80. This compared favourably with Paavo Nurmi's best time

Aarne Rita enjoying a sunny autumn day in his retirement years on the sauna verandah at Surprise Lake camp in 1987 (From the collection of Pentti Junni)

Yrjö Vala and Aarne Rita of Kiri

Yrjö Vala shows his fine form.

of 4:10:40 for the same distance around that time. In 1934 Yrjö Vala was chosen as a member of the Canadian team at the British Empire Games, taking part in javelin and shot put.

An article from the Kansallisseura files describes the eventual demise of Kiri as having been caused by the Great Depression, during which men had to go and find work wherever they could. Eventually the club folded for lack of interest.

Winter Sports

After the Surprise Lake camp was purchased, winter sports became a part of Kansallisseura activities, because the club now had an outdoor facility. A ski meet was held on March 19, 1961, followed by others in 1962 and 1963.

In 1964 the club organized a leisurely ski and sledding family day, and Väinö Mäkelä was asked to build a carousel for the event. What was it and was it ever built? *Laturetkiä* (cross-country ski tours) were held in 1965 and 1966, and downhill races in 1967. In 1968 *talkoohiihto*, which is assumed to have been a ski and work day, was the last recorded winter event at the camp.

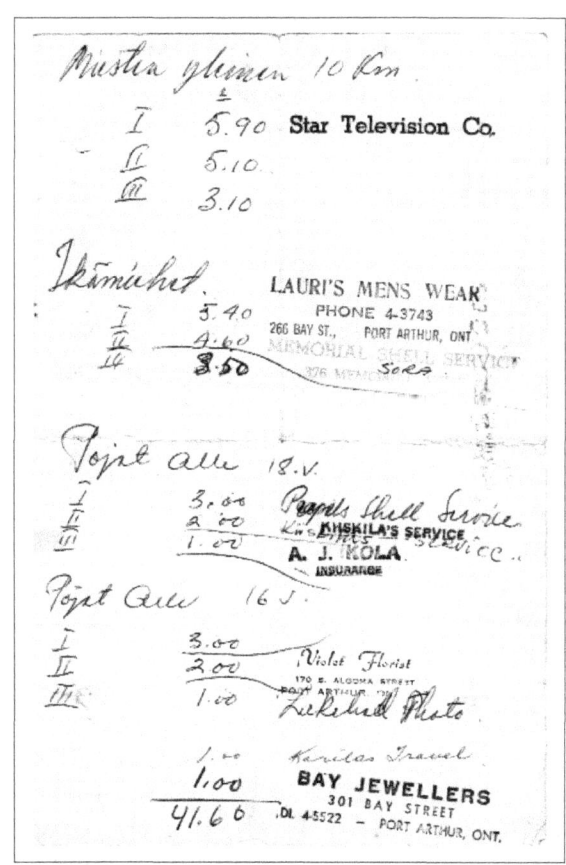

Events and their sponsors for the 1963 ski meet

Ski meet at Surprise Lake camp in the 1960s (From the collection of Pentti Junni)

In the mid 1960s Kansallisseura hosted an invitational ski meet for various Finnish clubs. *Keskipohjalaiset* (Ostrobothnians) took home the trophy, while the Otava Male Choir came in second and Kansallisseura, with Ilpo Ahokas, Pentti Junni and Vilho Ahokas, played the good host and came in last. All this sporting activity reflected the spirit of Kansallisseura, "to give the members an opportunity to develop their physical abilities".

Surprise Lake Swim

The Surprise Lake Swim, which started out as a fun competition in 1959 was, for 29 years, the central sporting activity at the Surprise Lake camp. The swim was the brainchild of Pauli Lumiala, one of the enthusiastic divers of this era. The first swim on August 16 had four men and four women taking part. A goodly number of spectators gathered to witness the races, which were 2.5 miles for men and ¾ mile for women.

By 1961 the roster of contestants had increased to six women and seven men vying for the trophies. Two of the ladies, Barbara Thompson and Sharon Coghlan failed to finish, but the others can be identified in the photo on page 87.

The distances varied from year to year, ranging from 2.5 miles to 1500 metres for men and from ¾ mile to 1000 metres for women. Only once, in 1960, did the women swim the same 2.5 mile distance as the men. All these inconsistencies make it impossible to compare the times from year to year, although careful records were kept and are available in the archives.

Participants of the first Surprise Lake Swim in 1959. In the back row from left to right are Teuvo Sorvisto – 2nd, Mikko – 4th, Håkan Carlson – 3rd, and Raili Parviainen - 3rd . Kneeling in the front row are Marjatta Lumiala – 2nd, Mårten Carlson – 1st, Anita Carlson – 1st, and Ines Parviainen – 4th (From the collection of Marjatta Ylikorpi)

Participants of the third Surprise Lake Swim in 1961. From left to right: Pauli Lumiala – official, Tuula Paalanen – 4th, Ulla Jämsä – 3rd, Sirkka Wahlberg – 2nd, Terttu Vuorinen – 1st, Dieter Bommes – 1st, Jack Gurney Sr. – 2nd, Pekka Kuisma – 3rd, Kaj Wickström – 4th, Teuvo Sorvisto – 5th, and Voitto Ylikorpi – official (From the collection of Pentti Junni)

In 1966 challenge trophies were added for men and women, to be presented permanently to three-time winners. The first trophy for women was donated by Salonen's Esso Service, and in 1971 Diana Humphreys took it home for keeps. She started the tradition of donating the women's trophy for the next round. The Diana Humphreys Challenge Trophy was permanently won in 1976 by Kathy MacLeay, and her trophy was taken home for keeps in 1981 by Wendy Nojonen.

In 1986 the Wendy Nojonen Challenge Trophy was won by 12-year old Wendy Rissanen, seated in the picture on p. 88, front row right. The previous year as an 11-year old she came in 4th, and won again in 1987, the last year the race was held. Thus she should have inherited the last women's challenge trophy. Beside Wendy in the photo is young Glen Halvorson, who was only 11 years old, but came in 2nd in the men's division.

The first trophy for the men's challenge cup was donated by Biltrite Lumber Company and was permanently won in 1971 by Roger Williams. The second trophy was donated by Vic Laurin Landscaping and was taken home for keeps in 1981 by Jim Donahue.

No further challenge trophies were donated for men. Thus by the time Bill Boswell came on the scene in 1978, and won the Surprise Lake Swim in 1982, 1984 and 1987, there was no challenge trophy to give him. Pat Hogan, on the other hand, had won the race three times in the years *before* the challenge trophy was introduced.

Vic Laurin, on the right, who donated the second men's challenge cup, handing the trophy to the winner of a Surprise Lake Swim in the 1970s (From the collection of Pentti Junni)

The most enthusiastic participants were found among the Senior Men, who competed from 1968 until the end in 1987. Unto Patvio shone by competing in 18 swims between 1961 and 1985, winning four times. Next came Jack Gurney Sr. with twelve, and Peter Rutherford with eleven entries in men's and senior men's categories. Other frequent entrants were Bill Boswell, Kaj Wickström and Diana Humphreys with eight swims, and Jari Lind and Wendy Nojonen with six. Jari set a new record as an 11-year old at his first swim meet in the men's open in 1974. The youngest competitors in the women's division were two 10-year old girls, Eija Ranta in 1968, (although she didn't finish) and Caryn Charban in 1986. In some years special categories for children were added, when the number of young participants warranted it.

In the years between 1963 and 1966 high diving competitions were included, until the diving tower became too shaky and its use was discontinued—at least in competitions. The winners of this event were Al McCormick in 1963, Jack Gurney Sr. in 1965, and Peter Bodnar in 1966.

Games and competitions were always available for the non-swimmers, with beanbag throw, air rifle shooting and darts being the most popular ones. For these events Finnish businesses often donated prizes: $5.00 gift card from Eaton's, mirror from Matson Hardware, flashlight from Midwest Auto, and one year The Finnish Book Store gave a doll named Raili for a raffle. Names of the winners

Participants of the 1986 Surprise Lake Swim: Sr. Men: Peter Rutherford – 1st; Ladies: Wendy Rissanen – 1st, Lorraine Dika – 2nd, Carrie Charban – 3rd, Joanne Boulter – 4th, Debbie Ritchie – 5th, Caryn Charban – 6th; Men: Ken Paradis – 1st, Glen Harvorson – 2nd, Todd Stock – 3rd, Ken Björn – 4th, Robert Kavanagh – 5th, Bill Boswell – 6th, Grant Mitchell – 7th, Victor Ritchie – 8th, Kevin Kennedy – 9th, Kim Hutch – 10th, Doug Niemi – 11th and Jari Leinonen – 12th (Not all pictured) (From the collection of Pentti Junni)

25. VUOTUINEN SURPRISE-JÄRVEN UINTI
Sunnuntaina, 10.7.1983 alkaen kello 13.30—

Lähtö ja maali Kansallisseuran kämpällä
Sarjat: miehet, naiset, ikämiehet (35 ja yli)
Ilmoittautuminen kämpällä tai puhelimilla 344-8516 tai 767-7298

ennen kilpailuja

MOJAKKAPÄIVÄLLINEN kämpällä alkaen klo 12.30
Kahvia — Hot Dogs — Virvokkeita
Kenttäpelejä kämpällä koko iltapäivän
KAIKKI TERVETULLEITA! Kansallis…

#27 — 09. heinäkuuta, 1980, CANADAN UUTISET

SURPRISE JÄRVEN UINTI
PIDETÄÄN SUNNUNTAINA, 20. HEINÄKUUTA

Miesten sarjan lähtö klo 13 (1 p.m.) järven alkupäästä.
Naisten ja Ikämiesten lähtö klo 13.15 sillalta.
Ilmoittautua voi kilpailupaikalla puoli tuntia ennen lähtöä. Ennakko-ilmoittautumiset ja tiedustelut puh. 344-8516 tai 767-2178.

PÄIVÄLLISET
Kansallisseuran kämpällä samana päivänä alkaen klo 12
Laatikoita ja Karjalan paistia.
Kämpällä myös lasten uintia ja kenttäpelejä.
JÄRJESTÄÄ KANSALLISSEURA   KAIKKI TERVETULOA!

Lind Cracks Swim Record

The Annual Surprise Lake Swim was held Sunday with swimmers in three classes competing. In the men's 2½ mile event Jari Lind, a mere 11 years old, not only won but set a new record in 51 minutes and 45 seconds. Runner-up Pete Rutherford at 54:35 was also under the old mark while Mark Illady finished third in 56:25. Last year's winner, Jack Gurney Jr., had to drop out because of breathing difficulties.

A casserole dinner and some other sports events for the spectators preceded the race. The event was sponsored by the Finnish National Society.

Winning the Ladies Open ¾-mile event was Kathy MacLeay and the Senior Men's ¾-mile Jack Gurney Sr.

Ladies Open ¾-Mile — Kathy MacLeay 18:15; Jocelyn Wilkins 25:23; Carol Johnson 25:24; Elja Ranta 28:19; Kaija Ranta 31:08; Heather Lauder 33:3.

Senior Men's ¾-Mile — Jack Gurney Sr. 31:19; Eepu Aksela 32:52; Tapio Paalanen 41:00; Unto Patvio 42:48.

CHRONICLE-JOURNAL 30/7/74

SURPRISE JÄRVEN 'OLYMPIALAISTEN' tulokset: 1976

UINTI

Miehet
1. Jim Donahue 40.05
2. Jari Lind 40.05
3. Mark Illady 47.23
4. Raymond Ranta 1.08.47

Naiset
1. Kathy MacLeay 15.15
2. Susan Johnson (10) 18.50
3. Carol Johnson (12) 19.25
4. Wendy Nojonen 23.25
5. Kaija Ranta 31.15

Ikämiehet
1. Unto Patvio (54) 38.45

KENTTÄPELIT

Ilmakivääriammunta
1. K. Toiviainen .... 44 p.
2. P. Junni .... 42 p.
3. A. Pasto .... 41 p.

Nuolenheitto
1. M. Vehniä .... 39 p.

Memories of the Surprise Lake Swim over its 29-year history

People ready to cheer the incoming swimmers at a Surprise Lake Swim in the 1970s (From the collection of Pentti Junni)

and participants of these *kenttäpelit* (field events) were recorded for posterity in the club books.

A scrumptious potluck dinner was served from about 1963 on by the Women's Club for a moderate price. It usually consisted of various home-made casseroles, jello, hot dogs, or *lihamojakka* (meat soup). A record book from 1963 gives an example of the delicious dishes prepared by the Kansallisseura women for the swim meets:

Aino Tiihonen	Spaghetti
Anna Erkkilä	Liver casserole
Aili Jaakkola	Carrot casserole
Tyyne Karttunen	Turnip casserole
A. Gohlin	Cabbage casserole
Ellen Ranta	Macaroni casserole
Tilda Tuomi	Meat casserole
Irene Suline	Meatballs
Reetta Junni	Macaroni casserole
Laila Mäkelä	Meat/potato casserole
Signe Peltola	Meat/potato casserole
Kirsti Wiitala	Cabbage casserole
Eeva Sora	Liver casserole
Marjatta Ylikorpi	Macaroni casserole
Liisa Lumiala	Herring
Ellen Poutanen	Shepherd's pie
Ines Parviainen	Five loaves of bread
Vera Jacobson	Jello
Toini Jacobson	Cabbage and turnip casseroles

In 1960 a 25¢ admission fee to the grounds was introduced to help cover the cost of the trophies. Over the years many local businesses also made donations, including Lauri's Men's Wear, Superior Motors, Saasto's Men's Wear, Finnport, Scandinavian Deli, Lauri's Hardware, Hoito Restaurant, Kangas Sauna, Anderson Block and Tile, Superior Lumber, Gateway Builders, Jacobson Lumber, Aurora Sales, Aho Jewelers, Lakehead Photo, Eino's Electrical Supplies, Kivelä Bakery, and James Murphy Oil.

In 1967 each swimmer received a Centennial Medal in honour of Canada's 100th birthday. Unusually low water levels in 1974 made it impossible for the participants to swim under the bridge. They had to get out of the water and sprint across the road, to the amusement of the spectators.

The club was always looking for extra boats to monitor the swimmers in the water. It was fortunate that no mishap ever occurred over the years, although on the 1969 swim results page someone had noted that one swimmer "...*jäi sillalla pois eikä maalissa tiedetty mitä hänelle tapahtui.*" (...dropped off at the bridge and at the finish they didn't

> Release
>
> I the undersigned understand that Finnish National Society, the organizer of the Surprise Lake Swim do not carry an Insurance policy covering, in any part, my personal wellbeing. Therefore I unconditionally release the organization of any liability and I accept that I enter the race on my own responsibility
>
> at Surprise Lake, Sunday July 13th 1986

Release form signed by the swimmers in 1986

know what happened to him.) St. John Ambulance was always present, but there was no insurance to cover the swimmers. It was not until 1986 that the competitors were required to sign a waiver releasing the club from any responsibility.

In 1986 the executive began to ponder whether it was time to end the swim. The prizes were getting too expensive and a $5.00 entry fee for swimmers was considered. At the executive meeting on February 18, 1988, the matter was again discussed. The workload was getting too onerous for the few people who had to carry all the responsibility. As it turned out, because the chairman, Pentti Junni, was in Finland, the executive decided against holding the swim that summer. So, after 29 years, the 1987 meet became the last one for this long-running competition that had started out as just a fun summer race in 1959.

Appendix II - "Surprise Lake Swim Results" contains a complete record of the names of all participants and their standings in this annual event for the years 1959 to 1987.

---

[1] *Canadan Uutiset,* May 29, 1930.
[2] Undated taped interview with Mr. Aarne Rita and Mrs. Vieno Rita by Pentti Junni.

Women's Activities

A group of Port Arthur Kansallisseura women decided at the September 2, 1926 meeting to start a *Käsityökerho* (Needlecraft Club), the purpose of which was to knit and sew articles for sale to support Kansallisseura activities. Mrs. K. Justin, Mrs. Helmi Lassi, Mrs. Ida Virtanen and Mrs. Edit Koivukoski were chosen as members of the first executive committee. This club existed intermittently for almost 30 years, organizing many fundraising events such as the ever-popular social evenings. The women also held bake sales, craft sales, and even a midsummer celebration at the Anderson cottage at Surprise Lake in 1937.

In 1932 the Needcraft Club hosted a special coffee party to raise money for the Finnish team going to the Los Angeles Olympics. The event was a great success and made a profit of $10.30, which was excellent, considering that the price of admission to these evenings was usually

Four hard-working Kansallisseura women from the early years: Mrs. Tilda Tuomi, Mrs. Salonen, Mrs. Ellen Poutanen and Mrs. Irene Suline (Photo from Kansallisseura archives)

twenty-five cents.

On March 7, 1933 the ladies organized a social evening with violin virtuoso Mr. Armas Laakso performing. It was very well received, especially with Mr. Lauri Korolainen providing a bit of comic relief, telling stories in the Savo dialect.

The lottery social held by the women on March 23, 1933 was an exceptional money-maker, generating a profit of $95.42. The hall was filled to overflowing with almost 500 people, preventing some from seeing the play "*Kihlaus*" ("The Engagement"). The highlight of the evening was the lottery, where the prizes included "an overcoat from Nelson-Kyrö, won by Mr. L.A. Mäki; a perm worth $6.50 from Savo-Vuori Beauty Parlour, won by Mrs. E. Jacobson; a cord of wood from Wanson and Töyrä, won by Mrs. S. Marttola; a beautiful pillow made by Mrs. Kyrö, won by Mrs. Karlson; and a ham from Bay Street Meat Market, won by Mrs. Ketonen."[1]

The Depression had an effect on Kansallisseura activities, as many men had to leave to look for work outside Port Arthur. However, the women kept busy, holding meetings at the homes of Mrs. Helmi Lassi, Mrs. L.A. Mäki, Mrs. Ida Virtanen, Mrs. William Oikonen, Mrs. Hanna Korolainen, Mrs. Edit Koivukoski, Mrs. Niilo Kyrö, Mrs. Lindquist, and at the Poutanen farm, where they had a sauna. During the fall of 1933, many members attended sewing bees, where they busily stitched garments that they distributed to the needy on December 21.

On March 28, 1934 the Needlecraft Club decided to perk things up by holding a Grand Masquerade evening. But generally, in the ensuing years, business within Kansallisseura was very quiet until 1939, when the club joined forces with other Finnish organizations to establish *Suomen Avustusyhdistys* (The Finnish Aid Society). It was the women who were major contributors to all fundraising efforts, as described in more detail in "Charitable Work" on page 70.

The Kansallisseura Needlecraft Club, as such, did not exist in the late 1930s and 1940s, because the women were involved with the church and the Finnish war effort. Then on October 8, 1951 the club had another "first" meeting. The eight women decided to gather at each other's homes every two weeks to make crafts, which would then be donated to Kansallisseura for sale. It was "decreed" that a hostess "...*sai tarjota vain kahta lajia leivoksia*" (...could serve only two kinds of baking). This rule prevented hostesses from getting too competitive with their coffee table offerings. The club was re-named *Kansallisseuran Naisten Kerho* (Kansallisseura Women's Club) and held social evenings and dances to raise money to buy materials for the various crafts they would make. The following list from the March 5, 1952 meeting at Mrs. Mannila's house gives an idea of the kinds of crafts made by Kansallisseura women:

Alma Pärssinen and Hanna Korolainen knit socks
Helli Viljakainen sewed a child's dress and a blouse
Vieno Tuomela sewed a satin pillow and a woman's cotton dress, and knit socks
Toini Parviainen knit short socks, and a baby's pink sweater and bonnet
Mrs. Tennant and Mrs. Forsberg crocheted doilies
Lilli Hendrickson donated crocheted items
Mrs. A. Saxberg sewed two aprons
Helmi Tolvanen made potholders
Mrs. Hämäläinen knit a child's wool sweater
Kirsti Viitala crocheted pansy doilies
Irene Suline knit a pair of socks

The club was again disbanded in 1953, but a receipt book from the archives shows that another version of

Mrs. Toini Jacobson serving food to Jouko Tuomialho and others at a summer event at Surprise Lake camp (From the collection of Pentti Junni)

Kansallisseura women: Vieno Rita, Toini Parviainen, Tilda Tuomi, Kirsti Viitala and Taimi Parviainen (From the collection of Toini Parviainen)

Käsityökerho operated from February, 1962 until November, 1965. The book records the profits from the coffee tables at the monthly meetings held at members' homes. The hostesses included Vera Jacobson, Laila Mäkelä, Marjatta Ylikorpi, Tilda Tuomi, Tyyne Karttunen, Anna Erkkilä, Kirsti Viitala, Ellen Poutanen, Hilja Lankinen, and Anna Liisa Vesterinen. In the late 1960s the club began operating as *Kansallisseuran Naiset* (Kansallisseura Women). For the next three decades the main activity for the women was to provide *laatikkopäivälliset*

Four hard-working Kansallisseura women from the later years: Reetta Junni, Raili Vänskä, Pirkko Tuisku and Sinikka Särkkä (From the collection of Pentti Junni)

(potluck dinners) for the Surprise Lake swim and food for Midsummer dances.

In fact, whenever food was needed, the women were involved. Thus events such as bake sales, picnics, turkey dinners, banquets, Christmas parties, film and coffee evenings, and spring clean-ups at Surprise Lake camp kept the women busy.

Whether it was collecting articles for rummage sales or *kirpputorit* (flea markets), buying presents for children's Christmas parties, running lotteries and bingos, or decorating halls for dances, it can be said with conviction that women were the real work force behind most Kansallisseura functions.

---

[1] *Canadan Uutiset*, April 5, 1933.

Youth Groups

Port Arthur Kansallisseura was always looking for new, young members, to continue the work of the organization as the "old-timers" began to lose steam.

Finnish Canadian Club (1947 – 1950)

Kansallisseura had already functioned for over twenty years and the founding members felt that new blood was needed to bring more energy to the club.

At the January 9, 1947 annual meeting there was much discussion about starting a youth group, which was done forthwith. This new group, known as *Kansallisseuran Nuorten Kerho* (Finnish Canadian Club), was led by Kai Koivukoski, who was carrying on his father's tradition—Mr. Kosti Koivukoski having been one of Kansallisseura's founding members.

In April this new club organized its first dance at the Sons of England Hall[1].

> "This Youth Club was only recently started and many members have already joined. Now that these young people of ours are holding their first social evening, it would behoove us, older folk, to attend and thus give them our full support. In this way we will encourage the young people to continue their activities. Naturally the program will be light, with many novelties worth seeing and hearing. At the end there will be dancing under coloured lights. The young people will try out a new orchestra that is reputed to be excellent."

Vic Blazina Orchestra, among others, now provided the kind of music the younger people preferred. In October they

Article from Canadan Uutiset, reporting on the new Finnish Canadian Club

Ad for Finnish Canadian Club dance in 1948

played at a dance held by the club at the Italian Hall. At this time Eric Peterson was the chairman, with Tauno Ketonen as vice-chairman.

Nineteen forty-nine was a busy year for the Finnish Canadian Club. In April, they organized a variety evening and a dance, with tickets selling for 45¢, with 50¢ at the door. A dance in August generated a profit of $98.40[2].

"This sum was sent to CARE office in Ottawa for the purpose of purchasing food parcels, which they sent to needy school children in Finland.

We have received personal letters from these children, in which they thank us for the food packages they received. Most of these letters are from Helsinki, and were written in English.

Our club also assembled and sent 46 Christmas gift packages to all children up to 15 years of age in the Fort William Sanatorium. These packages contained oranges, apples, nuts, candies, chocolate bars and chewing gum, as well as few dozen magazines and books.

A magazine subscription was sent to a young Finnish boy who has been in a Port Arthur convalescent hospital for several years.

A Valentine dance will be held at the Italian Hall on February 15 and we expect many people to come and spend a delightful evening."

Aside from fundraising, the youth group's main activity was bowling, and

Article in Canadan Uutiset *by Vice-Chairman T.J. Ketonen, describing the Finnish Canadian Club's activities in 1949*

their 1950 season ended with an enjoyable dinner at Highland Inn restaurant. The team called Strikers won the trophy presented by Mr. Saasto. Several other trophies and "presents" were handed out to deserving bowlers.

The club held its fourth annual concert at the Italian Hall on May 23, 1950. The program was varied and the audience was very satisfied with all it had seen and heard. That year the club donated $25.00 to Manitoba flood relief. On November 22, 1950 the Finnish Canadian Club changed its name to Athletics, Charity and Entertainment (A.C.E). It was at this point that they probably became an independent charitable organization and separated from Kansallisseura.

Nor-Shor Club (1957 – 1962)

For a few years there was no young people's group within Port Arthur Kansallisseura. However, it appears that discussions had been going on early in 1956 for its establishment. At that time Mr. L. Tulkku was in charge of the Sudbury Sampo young people, whose help had been solicited for Kansallisseura's 30th anniversary celebration.

He wrote in one of his letters, *"Mainitsemastani kokouksesta meidän käsitys olis että sinne seuranne yhteyteen perustettaisiin samanlainen kerho kun mitä meillä täällä Sudburissa on—Sammon Pojat. Ehkä sillä tavalla saisitte nuoria mukaan. Ja meidän nuoret tulisi kokouksessa selostamaan toimintoamme täällä Sudburissa mikä sopisi sinne teille myös."* (From the meeting I was referring to, we got the impression that you were planning to establish, within your organization, a club such as the one we have here in Sudbury—Sampo Boys. Perhaps in this way you could get young people involved. And at your meeting our young people could come and tell about their activities here in Sudbury, which would also be suitable for you over there.)

Also at the

Teuvo Sorvisto, Pauli Lumiala and Veijo Parviainen clowning on stage at a social evening in Nipigon in 1958 (From the collection of Marjatta Ylikorpi)

July 2, 1956 meeting of the Central Organization of Loyal Finns in Canada (COLFC) in Montreal, the need for getting young people involved with sports,

Nor-Shor Club dancers performing in Nipigon in 1958. Counter-clockwise from middle front: Håkan Carlson and Ulla Jämsä, Raili Parviainen and Reino Erkkilä, Mårten Carlson and partner, Kaarina Parviainen and Lasse Peltola, Olavi Laine and Anita Carlson (From the collection of Marjatta Ylikorpi)

theatre, gymnastics, etc. was highlighted. All branches of Kansallisseura were encouraged to hold open discussions about this issue.

Then in 1957 Pauli Lumiala moved from Toronto to Port Arthur with his wife, Liisa, and daughter, Marjatta. They joined Kansallisseura and, not long after, Pauli was instrumental in organizing a youth group called Nor-Shor Club. The club soon gained a number of enthusiastic members who began to practice Finnish folk dancing at the Western Bearcat Hall on Clark Street. When Pekka Kuisma, an accomplished accordionist came from Finland and joined the group, he provided authentic Finnish music for the folk dancers, as well as for the numerous social evenings and dances Kansallisseura held during the next few years.

At the February 24, 1958 meeting the chairman of Nor-Shor Club, Voitto Ylikorpi, announced that the folk dancers would be performing at a social evening in Nipigon, organized by Otava Male Choir later in the spring.

The fun-filled evening brought in a profit of $47.90. This was the first performance where the men wore their new vests, sewn from fabric that was ordered from Seinäjoki, Finland by Mrs. Linden.

That summer Nor-Shor Club took part for the first time in folk dancing competitions at *Suurjuhlat* (Finnish Canadian Grand Festival), held that year in Port Arthur.

In March of 1959 six members of Nor-Shor Club drove to Sudbury for a work shop in preparation for the combined folk dances to be performed by groups from around Ontario at *Suurjuhlat* in Timmins. In addition to the combined folk dances, Nor-Shor club took part in the competition, performing "*Tuliluikka*",

Bill from Seinäjoki, Finland, for fabric, pattern and buttons for men's folk dance vests

Nor-Shor Club folk dancers in 1958 at Suurjuhlat *in Port Arthur. From left to right: Anna Erkkilä, Lasse Peltola, Kaarina Parviainen, Toivo Erkkilä, Helena Luomala, Olavi Laine, Marjatta Lumiala, Voitto Ylikorpi, Raili Parviainen, Reino Erkkilä, Raili Nuutinen and Pentti Mäkelä, with Pekka Kuisma and his accordion in front (From the collection of Marjatta Ylikorpi)*

accompanied on the piano by Väinö Jacobson Jr. Although the group had spent countless hours rehearsing in the old Surprise Lake log cabin, they failed to take first prize. However, the following year at *Suurjuhlat* in Sudbury, Nor-Shor Club won the competition with Pekka Kuisma playing "*Sappo*" on his accordion.

Liisa Lumiala had been involved with the Sisu little girls' rhythmic gymnastics in Toronto, and she now organized a similar group within Kansallisseura. The little girls performed at *Suurjuhlat* in 1959 in Timmins in their new gym outfits, sewn by Mrs. Gerda Carlson.

On June 20, 1959, at the second annual *Juhannus* (Midsummer) celebration, held at Surprise Lake camp, Nor-Shor Club participated for the first time. They introduced the election of a Miss *Juhannus* by audience vote, and Anita Carlson won hands down. That same year Nor-Shor Club performed folk dances on local TV, and on Boxing Day the club held a very successful dinner-dance at the Fort William Golf and Country Club.

The May Day dinner-dance on April 30, 1960 at the same location was also very well attended. The Nor-Shor girls made *vappuhuiskia* (May Day pom-poms) for sale, giving the club a financial boost of $16.00. However, by 1962 most of the Nor-Shor Club members had dispersed to their various life callings.

Liisa Lumiala at Western Bearcat Hall with the Nor-Shor Club little girl gymnasts, including Marjaana Jämsä, Paula Laitinen, Lea Parviainen, Elisa Korpela, Sinikka Hartikainen, Aina Kojola, Aila Tiitto, Sirkka-Liisa Laakso and Pirjo Hoffren (From the collection of Marjatta Ylikorpi)

These young ladies are ready for a dance at the Boxing Day event in 1959. From left to right: Unknown, Kaarina Lehtonen, Anita Carlson, Brenda Buick, Raili Parviainen and Marjatta Lumiala (From the collection of Marjatta Ylikorpi)

Nor-Shor Club Dancers (1964 – 1971)

Youth club activities were in hiatus until 1964 when, at a meeting on August 18, Eva Sora told about a group of young people who were interested in joining Nor-Shor Club and learning to folk dance. Kansallisseura decided to help, and so Eva and Laila Mäkelä organized these young people, mainly from the Jumbo Gardens High School area, under the name of Nor-Shor Club Dancers. Anna Erkkilä taught folk dances to the group until she left for Finland, at which point Penni Junni took over the job. Ten

Pentti Junni, Pirjo Lampo, Reijo Ranta-Ojala, Marja-Leena Arnam, Glen Paavola, Eeva-Liisa Suvanto, Teuvo Mutka, Arja Lampo, Lasse Tuomialho and a visitor from Finland at Sault Ste. Marie Suurjuhlat in 1966 (From the collection of Pentti Junni)

Nor-Shor Club Dancers on their way to Winnipeg in December, 1967. From left to right: Pirjo Lampo, Glen Paavola, Marja-Leena Arnam, Pentti Junni, Olavi Vesterinen, Liisa Vesterinen, Lasse Tuomi-aho with Reijo Ranta-Ojala in front (From the collection of Pentti Junni)

members participated in the combined folk dances at the Sault Ste. Marie *Suurjuhlat* in 1966, receiving $36.82 for their efforts.

Nineteen sixty-seven, Canada's Centennial year, was a very busy one for the youth club. They participated at Centennial celebrations in Marathon, Terrace Bay and Thunder Bay, and also entertained residents at Dawson Court Seniors' Home and Ontario Hospital. Along with a number of ethnic clubs, they attended the Folklorama '67 at the Exhibition Grandstand, performing "*Säkkijärven Polkka*" and "*Saaristo Polska*", accompanied by Pentti Hirvonen, Pauli Arvo and Olavi Vesterinen. A "sauna-like deluge" failed to dampen their spirits, a fact that was acknowledged in a thank-you letter from the organizers as follows: "Your generous spirit in proceeding with the production in spite of pouring rain has endeared you and your group, not only to us of the Folk Arts Council, but also to all the citizens who were privileged to be in attendance that night." The young people finished off the year by flying to Winnipeg to dance at another Folk Arts Festival.

The club took part in an ethnic event at the Lakehead University in 1970, where Nor-Shor Club Dancers in colourful folk costumes presided over a display of various articles of Finnish design. That summer they also danced and sang in Tapiola at *Juhannus*.

Eeva-Liisa Suvanto and Pirjo Lampo at Lakehead University in 1970 with a display of Finnish wares (From the collection of Pentti Junni)

This group of young people did not only entertain, but they also exhibited empathy towards fellow club members, as shown by this note found in the files:

In April, 1967 Nor-Shor Club Dancers donated $5.00 to the funeral assistance fund for Ranta-Ojala's child.

Nor-Shor Club Dancers also performed with the newly formed Kiikurit, Finlandia Club folk dancers, led by Martti Vanhapelto, who had recently immigrated from Kuopio, Finland. With this performance, Nor-Shor Club "gave the stage" to Kiikurit, since studies, work and marriage had taken their toll on the membership. It was suggested at a January 17, 1971 meeting that Nor-Shor Club should officially be disbanded.

For the last thirty years Kansallisseura did not have enough young people at any one time to form another youth group. Since the older people were no longer willing or able to contribute time and effort into Kansallisseura's activities, this absence of youthful energy was one of the contributing factors to the eventual demise of the club.

Sinikka Vataja, Anja Hankilanoja with Anja Junni, Rainer Partanen, Kaisa Kolehmainen with Helena Junni, Lasse Tuomialho, Marjaana Jämsä and Pirkko Kraft at Tapiola at Juhannus, 1970 (From the collection of Pentti Junni)

---

[1] *Canadan Uutiset*, March 26, 1947.
[2] *Canadan Uutiset*, January 11, 1950.

Noteworthy Members

Although in the ranks of Port Arthur Kansallisseura many industrious people served over the years, it is important to give special mention to some individuals, who were instrumental in furthering the club's aims in a most dedicated manner.

Founding Members

Based on existing Kansallisseura records, it has been estimated that there were approximately 34 people at the founding meeting on January 22, 1926. The twenty-nine names that have been identified as possible Founding Members are shown below:

Honorary Members

Over the years, seventeen people in Port Athur Kansallisseura were given the distinction of being named Honorary Members. This recognition was granted to those who had proven themselves worthy by contributing to the club's activities "above and beyond the call of duty". The *Kunniakirja* (Certificate of Honour) documents their niche in the Kansallisseura "Hall of Fame" for posterity.

The first Honorary Member was Mr. Kosti Koivukoski, who was named Honorary Chairman in 1931, when he retired as Chairman. *Siirtolainen,* the 1933 Christmas publication of Kansallisseura,

Elsa Autio	H. W. Niinimäki
Eeli Hendrickson	Vieno Paananen
Lilli Hendrickson	Väinö Pentti
Vera Jacobson	Vieno Rita
Walter Jacobson	Alfred Saxberg
Sanni Kallio	Mrs. A. Saxberg
Edit Koivukoski	Yrjö Saxberg
Kosti Koivukoski	R. Schrey
Erick J. Korte	Irene Suline
Hilja Korte	Olli Tikkanen
Niilo Kyrö	Matilda Tuomi
Maiju Leinonen	Martha Vertanen
Lauri Maunu	Ida Virtanen
Leonard W. Mäki	Kalle Virtanen
Tyyne Mäki	

Certificate of Honour awarded to twelve Honorary members in 1964 by Port Arthur Kansallisseura

contained a write-up on the two other people who had become Honorary Members that year.

"During this year our Kansallisseura gave the rank of Honorary Member to Mrs. Ida Virtanen, to show our gratitude even in this humble way for the work she has done on behalf of our Kansallisseura. Mrs. I. Virtanen has a *'roominki talo'* (rooming house) on Secord Street, which has, for a long time, been known especially to White men…There Kansallisseura was able to plan its rules in peace. Mrs. I. Virtanen has, during the whole time the club has existed, taken part in club activities with enthusiasm, having been, for example, several years on the executive, and the chairman of the Needlecraft Club. She has hardly missed a single dance, where she has been the club's hostess. Mrs. Virtanen is one of those personalities who does her work quietly, without wanting her name singled out. Never has she been heard to complain about the amount of work, even though often responsibility for the whole club has been almost totally on her shoulders. With her example she has often encouraged and inspired many a younger member. She has organized many, many *'yllätys paartia'* (surprise parties), but have we ever gone to her house to thank her for her noble work on behalf of Kansallisseura?

On Secord Street is our third Honorary

```
Taman vuoden aikana kansallisseuramme antoi kunniajasenen arvon
Mrs. I. Virtaselle, osoitaakseen edes vahan kiitollisuuttaan ha-
nen tekemastaan tyosta kansallisseuramme hyvaksi. Mrs I. Wirta
selle jolla on roominki talo Secord kadulla joka jo kavan on ol-
lut tunnettu erittainkin valkoisille miehille. Silloin kun Suomen
vapaus-sota paattyi ja sen jalkimaininget vieryivat aina tanne
Kanadaan saakka jolloin taalla valkoisten ja punaisten suoma-
laisten valit olivat viela kireammat, kuin mita ne nyt ovat, niin
silloin hanen kotinsa oli Port Arthurissa ainut valkoisten suoma-
laisten turvpaikka. Sielle tunsi olevansa turvassa ja kotonaan.
Sielle kansallisseurakin sai rahassa saantojaan laatia. Mrs. I.
Tirtanen on koko seuran olomassaolon aikana ottanut innolla osaa
seuratoimintaan, ollut mm, useita vuosia johtokunnassa ja kasit-
yokerhon puheenjohtajana. Tuskinpa han lie monestakaan iltamasta
ollut pois, jossa han on toiminut seuran emantana. Mrs Wirtanen
on yksi niita luonteita, joka tekee hiljaista tyotansa, tahtomatt
tulla nimensa kuuluksi. Ei koskaan hanen ole viela kuultu valti-
tevan tyonpaljoutta, vaikka monasti koko seuran toiminta on ollut
melkein yksinomaan hanen harteillaan. Esimerkillaan han on monta
nuorempaa jasenta rohkaissut ja innostanut. Monelle, monelle on
taallakin pidetty yllatys "paartia", mutta olemmeko kertaakaa
hanen luonaan kaynset kiitamassa hanen jalosta tyostaan k. seuran
hyvaksi?
Secord kadulla meidan kolmas kunnia jasen, Mr. K. Toyra. Han on
myos yksi niita miehia, joka eit tehdo paastaa nimeaan kuuluksi,
vaan tekee seuran hyvaksi tyota kaisessa hiljaisuudessa, paljon
enempi kuin me tiedammekaan. Useita vuosia han on tunnon tark-
kaudella hoitanut seuran rahastonhoitajan tehtavan. Hoitaen nykyi-
sin myos keskusliiton rahavarat.
Lahes vuoden han oli myos seuran puheenjatajana, jonka paikan han
taytti kunnollisesti. Olisimme toivoneet, etta han edelleenkin
oli ollut seuran puheenjohtajana, mutta tyosuohteidensa takia han
joutui keskella vuotta ottamaan siita eron. Monessa seuraa kos-
kevassa kriitillisessa tilanteessa han on osannut antaa kultaisia
toiminta ohjeita, jotka ovat auttaneet.--
```

Article from Siirtolainen *on two honorary members from 1933*

Member, Mr. Kalle Töyrä. He is also one of those men who does not want his name brought out to the fore, but works on behalf of the club in silence much more than we know. For several years he has conscientiously held the office of the club's treasurer. Today he also takes care of the finances of the central organization. For almost a year he was also the club's chairman, which office he filled with honour. We would have wished for him to continue to be the club's chairman, but because of his work situation he had to resign in the middle of the year. In many critical situations concerning the club, he has known how to give golden directives, which have been helpful."

Two more Kansallisseura members received this honour in 1956 for their quarter-century of work in the club. Central Organization of Loyal Finns in Canada (COLFC) was asked to send two certificates, and so Irene Olga Suline received *Kunniakirja* #8 and Vera Maria Jacobson was given *Kunniakirja* #9. The last honours were handed out in 1964, when twelve more members received their honourary certificates. Although in the ensuing years there must have been many deserving members, no further certificates were handed out.

Based on existing records, the following list contains the names of all Honorary Members:

Toini Jacobson	1964
Väinö Jacobson	1964
Vera Maria Jacobson	1956
Tyyne Karttunen	1964
Kosti Koivukoski	1931
Ellen Poutanen	1964
Ralph Poutanen	1964
Saimi Rissanen	1964
Veikko Rissanen	1964
Aarne Rita	1964
Vieno Rita	1964
Irene Olga Suline	1956
Carl (Kalle) Töyrä	1933
Matilda Tuomi	1964
Kirsti Viitala	1964
Niilo Viitala	1964
Ida Virtanen	1933

The following three members have been chosen for special recognition to symbolize all the "unsung heroes" who made up the membership of Kansallisseura over the years. Kosti Koivukoski represents the beginning, Pentti Junni personifies the end, and Toini Jacobson stands for all the hardworking women, who were the backbone of the club.

Kosti Koivukoski

Mr. Kosti Koivukoski was the principal founder of the Kansallisseura movement in Canada, when he started Kansallisseura Turisti in Port Arthur in 1926. He was born in Perniö, Finland on February 5, 1890 and died on March 7, 1952 in Port Arthur. He came to Canada with his family in 1925 and immediately began to make his mark in the Finnish-Canadian circles. He served as chairman of Port Arthur Kansallisseura for the first five years, and later again in 1942, when the club was revived. He was given a lifetime membership and was named Honorary Chairman in 1931.

For a number of years he served on the executive of COLFC. In 1939 he was instrumental in establishing the Finnish Canadian Aid Society to help with the Finnish war effort. He also set up an office to help Finns find work, especially in the bush camps around Port Arthur, and as far away as Longlac.

A dedicated music man, over the years Mr. Koivukoski founded and conducted a number of choirs, including various church choirs, Sointu Mixed Choir, and Otava Mixed Choir. He entertained at most of the Kansallisseura social evenings, and his comic songs were a particular audience favourite.

Mr. Koivukoski was a very prolific speaker and it was a rare occasion when he did not orate on some topic. He gave lectures and speeches at many clubs and organizations, and also wrote about Finland and Finns on the pages of English-language newspapers.

In the early years Mr. Koivukoski's cottage provided Kansallisseura members with many enjoyable hours of relaxation by the lake. In a letter to the editor in *Canadan Uutiset* in 1932, Mr. Koivukoski was described as "*tunnettu, tarmokas, kyvykäs, vankka, horjumaton ja tosikansallismielinen*" (well-known, energetic, able, steady, unflinching, and a true nationalist). That pretty well summarized the man in the opinion of most people.

Pentti Junni

Pentti Junni was born on December 29, 1927 in Rautu, Karjala, Finland. His first sojourn in Canada as a bachelor was from 1952 to 1954, after which he returned to Finland. He immigrated for the second time to Port Arthur in 1958 with his wife, Reetta, and the first of three daughters. He worked as a mechanic until his retirement.

Pentti Junni is a musician and sings in the Otava Male Choir. He also played the violin for dance orchestras such as Pelimannit and Souvaripojat, which often supplied music for the Midsummer dances and *Humppatanssit* held by Kansallisseura at the Surprise Lake camp or Finlandia Club. He organized many Kansallisseura social evenings, where he sang solos, and duets with Eeva Sora. He is a song-writer and a published poet, and has collaborated on CDs with artists in Finland. His weekly radio program "*Sävelsilta*" ("*Musical Bridge*") has been a popular fixture in Port Arthur for over 45 years.

Pentti Junni joined Kansallisseura in 1960 and already the following year became the representative to COLFC. He was elected chairman in 1963 and for the next 39 years performed his duties with dedication. He served as the mainstay for the annual Surprise Lake Swim, organizing the myriad details for the event. This role became particularly crucial during the latter years, when the membership declined to a dozen or so active members. In 1988, when he went to Finland, the executive decided not to proceed with the Swim without his contribution, thus ending the 29-year run of this event.

Over the years Pentti has held leadership roles with the Thunder Bay Finnish Language School, Otava Male Choir, Finlandia Club and Finnish Canadian Grand Festival. He serves as a "lightning rod" into the Thunder Bay Finnish community, providing a connection for various individuals and organizations in Finland and North America. He is a popular and well-respected member of the community, as shown by the fact that his 50th birthday was attended by over 200 people.

Pentti Junni has a deep-rooted connection to his Finnish heritage and a strong commitment to maintaining Finnish culture in Thunder Bay and Canada.

Toini Jacobson

Mrs. Toini Jacobson was born at 217 St. James Street in Port Arthur, Ontario on November 8, 1910 and her name first emerged from the pages of Kansallisseura records in 1946. From that day forward, it appeared in the minutes whenever any event was organized. By 1950 she was a member of the executive and in 1958 took on the position of membership secretary. Mrs. Jacobson was an active member of the *Käsityökerho* (Needlecraft Club) in the early 1950s, serving as the secretary, and often opening her home for the meetings.

Although Mrs. Jacobson generally operated in the background, organizing events and working on various committees, her family was often "front and centre". Her husband Väinö sang, and her sons Onni and Väinö Jr. performed musical numbers at many Kansallisseura social evenings.

In 1960 Mrs. Jacobson was elected treasurer of Kansallisseura and served with dedication in that capacity for the next 23 years. During that time she became the keeper of the Kansallisseura records, faithfully storing every bill and receipt for posterity. To this diligence we owe many of the facts in this history, and without her foresight and attention to detail, this book would not have been possible.

The boxes of Kansallisseura records were clearly labeled "Upon my death, pass on to Pentti Junni."

Mrs. Jacobson passed away on February 15, 1992. In her cherished financial journals there is an entry. "Flowers for Toini Jacobson's funeral—$46.00".

"The Big Picture"

Although Port Arthur Kansallisseura operated within a small community of Finnish Canadians in Port Arthur (later Thunder Bay), its history was not untouched by world events. It owed its birth to the Red and White conflict, and to the nationalistic spirit that dominated Finnish politics after the country's independence. The Depression in the 1930s caused the club to direct its activities towards charitable work. During WWII, Kansallisseura set its sights on helping the old homeland. The Continuation War stamped Finnish Canadians as "enemy aliens", resulting in increased charitable activity towards Canadian and British organizations, and a greater show of loyalty to Canada. The increase in immigration in the 1950s gave Kansallisseura a welcome boost in membership, and led to the purchase of the Surprise Lake camp and the activity associated with it. Conversely as immigration slowed to a trickle, the membership declined to precarious levels in the mid 1980s, until it led to the inevitable demise of the club.

Kansallisseura and Finland

Several photographs of Finnish presidents were found in the Kansallisseura archives, indicating the strong nationalistic idealism of the founding members. The links to the old homeland were especially powerful during the terms of the following presidents.

Kaarlo Juho Ståhlberg
(1865 – 1952)
Term: 1919 – 1925

During his term a large influx of Finnish immigrants came to Canada, setting the stage for Kansallisseura's birth.

Lauri Kristian Relander
(1883 – 1942)
Term: 1925 – 1931

During his term Port Arthur Kansallisseura was established. The club was very active with social evenings and theatre, and was looking for a home.

Pehr Evind Svinhufvud
(1861 – 1944)
Term: 1931 – 1937

During his term Depression was at its peak and Kansallisseura was doing charitable work in the community. Activity in the club was waning.

Kansallisseura received the following thank you note on behalf of President Svinhufvud for the congratulatory telegram that was sent on the occasion of his 70th birthday on December 15, 1931.

"The President of the Republic has ordered the undersigned to express the President's warm gratitude for the congratulations he received from you on the occasion of his 70th birthday.

Respectfully,
L. Aström, Finnish Ambassador"

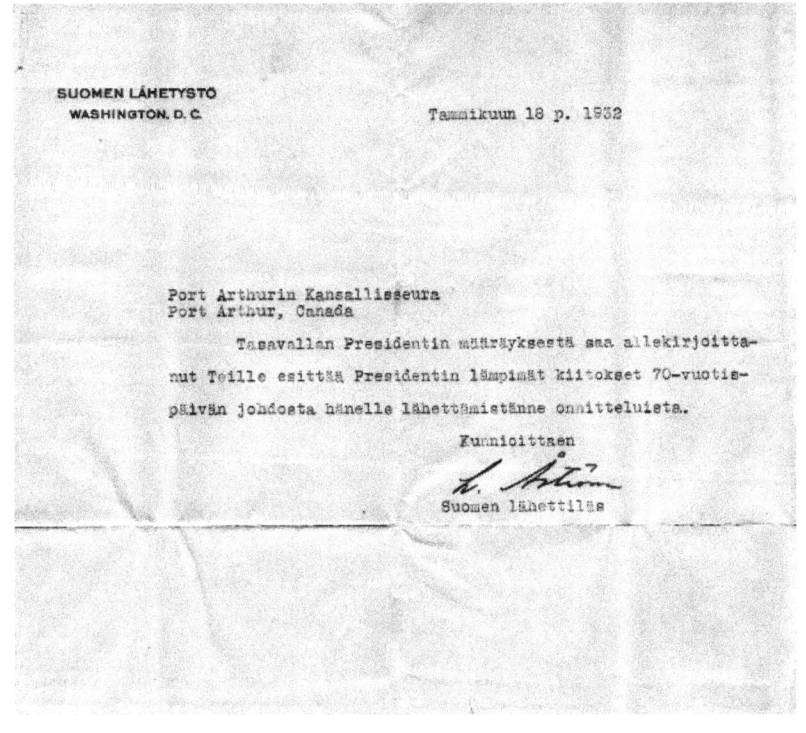

Kyösti Kallio
(1873 – 1940)
Term: 1937 – 1940

During his term Kansallisseura members were actively involved with Finnish Aid Society, raising money for the Finnish war effort. The club itself, however, was largely inactive.

Risto Heikki Ryti
(1889 – 1956)
Term: 1940 – 1944

President Risto Ryti led Finland throughout the difficult war years. During his term, Kansallisseura was revived and continued to raise funds for the Finnish war effort.

Carl Gustaf Emil Mannerheim
(1867 – 1951)
Term: 1944 – 1946

During his term Kansallisseura continued to do fundraising for Canada-Finland Aid Society Fund.

Juho Kusti Paasikivi
(1870 – 1986)
Term: 1946 – 1956

During his term Kansallisseura purchased the Surprise Lake camp and membership was growing.

Urho Kaleva Kekkonen
(1900 – 1986)
Term: 1956 – 1982

During his term Nor-Shor Club was established and membership peaked at over 100. The traditions of Surprise Lake Swim and Midsummer dance were started.

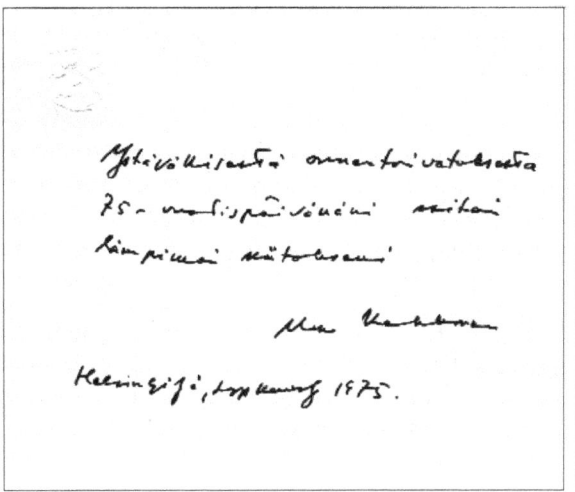

Kansallisseura received the above thank you note from President Kekkonen for the congratulatory telegram sent on his 75th birthday.

"For your friendly wishes for happiness on my 75th birthday, I send you my warm thanks.
Urho Kekkonen
Helsinki, September, 1975."

The Central Organization

Shortly after the establishment of Kansallisseura in Port Arthur, a number of similar nationalistic clubs were started in other locations. By 1931 there were ten organizations, including Toronto, which had begun on August 20, 1930 as Finnish National Society. Toronto felt it was time to establish a central unit, "to provide cohesion for the scattered nationalistic societies. The aims of the organization were to change the political image of the Finnish Canadians, to increase their employment opportunities and, eventually, to put an end to Finnish radicalism in Canada."[1]

Port Arthur felt it was too early for such an undertaking, but Toronto went ahead anyway, and the Central Organization of Loyal Finns in Canada (COLFC) was born on February 22, 1931. The Finnish name of the organization went through a number of changes, from the original *Kanadan Lojaalisten Suomalaisten Keskusliitto*, to *Kanadan Kansallis- ja Edistysseurojen Keskusjärjestö* in 1932, to *Kanadan Kansallismielisten Suomalaisten Liitto* in 1933, then in 1955, back to *Kanadan Lojaalisten Suomalaisten Keskus-Liitto*. In the 1959 annual meeting, the name was further shortened to *Canadan Suomalaisten Keskusliitto*. It is possible there were other versions in between.

"Overall, the membership in the Loyal Finns remained small. In 1936, after five years of active organizing, Finnish Vice-Consul F.A. Mustonen commented in *Kanadan Suomalainen*, a Loyal Finns' publication that the organization had only eighteen locals across Canada and about 500 members, half of whom were in Montreal. He continued: Even if we count the so-called supporters of our organization, those who attend our entertainment evenings and thus give us financial assistance, as ten times the official number of members, our organization has still never reached even 10 percent of the Finns in Canada."[2]

Other membership figures were reported in a *Port Arthur News-Chronicle* article from 1933, which stated that the Port Arthur branch had 200 members, and COLFC membership was nearly 2,000 and growing.

Reference has been found to the following locations containing branches of Loyal Finns in Canada:

British Columbia:
    Vancouver (*Valistus- ja Edistysseura Suomi* - 1928)

Alberta:
    Calgary
    Edmonton
    Radway (1932)
    Sylvan Lake (1933)

Saskatchewan:
    Regina
    Saskatoon

Manitoba:
    Winnipeg (*Winnipegin Kansallisseura* - 1931)

Ontario:
    Bruce Mines (1932)
    Copper Cliff
    Kirkland Lake (1931)
    Oshawa
    Port Arthur (*Port Arthurin Kansallisseura* - 1926)
    Sault Ste. Marie
    South Porcupine
    Sudbury (*Sudburyn Kansallisseura* - 1930)
    Timmins
    Toronto *(Toronton Suomalainen Kansallisseura* - 1930)
    Windsor (*Windsorin Suomi Seura*)

Quebec:
    Montreal (*Montrealin Suomi Seura* – 1927)

The Port Arthur branch had yet to join COLFC, but by the end of 1932 the central organization had moved there, with Mr. Kosti Koivukoski as its chairman. One of his first official acts was to exhort all member organizations to begin their preparations for the Finnish Independence Day on December 6. He concluded the letter by saying "Finland has the right to expect that her loyal sons and daughters in foreign lands will dedicate at least one evening a year totally to the distant, but always dear country of their mothers and fathers. Thus let it become a beautiful tradition that every branch will annually celebrate Finnish Independence Day."[3]

Port Arthur Kansallisseura had always felt that COLFC should be in Port Arthur, since it was the oldest club and was centrally located, but for some reason it didn't join the central organization until 1933.

In the mid 1930s the activity at the Port Arthur branch slowed down considerably, as described in "The Missing Years" on page 20. Thus it is not surprising to find that in 1936 COLFC moved to Montreal, where it resided for over 20 years. In 1958 COLFC made the final move to Sudbury, where its records were lost soon after in a devastating fire at Sampo Hall. Yet COLFC stayed there until it was disbanded in 1997.

Sometime after COLFC moved to Montreal, the Port Arthur branch stopped communicating with the organization. It did not pay its dues for many years, or even report its current address. It was not until 1954 that Port Arthur Kansallisseura felt the need to re-join COLFC, because the branch had misplaced the charter that made it legal.

By this time there were only about half a dozen active branches across Canada, with a total of approximately 500 members, as calculated from the membership fees collected by COLFC in 1958. Over the years the branches either

Certificate showing when Kansallisseura joined COLFC on April 18, 1933

evolved or died. The Vancouver branch, for example, is now Vancouver Finlandia Club, an umbrella organization for a number of Finnish clubs in the area. Their recent history is captured in an excellent book *Vancouver Finlandia Club: Uudet juuret—Uudet tuulet.*

"The most important contribution of the Loyal Finns in Canada was to provide an alternative platform of expression in many Finnish communities. Prior to the strengthening of Finnish Canadian religious institutions and prior to the non-political Finnish organizations that dominate the Finnish activity in Canada today, the Loyal Finns organized and successfully protected the White islands in the Red sea."[4]

---

[1] Lindstrom-Best, Varpu, "Central Organization of the Loyal Finns in Canada," *Polyphony: The Bulletin of the Multicultural History Society of Ontario, Finns in Ontario*, (Vol. 3, No. 2, Fall 1981) p. 97.
[2] Ibid., p. 101.
[3] Letter to Port Arthur Kansallisseura from COLCF Chairman Kosti Koivukoski, dated November 1, 1932.
[4] Lindstrom-Best, Varpu, "*Polyphony*", op. cit. p. 103.

The End

The lifeblood of an organization is its membership. When, for one reason or another, the level sinks too low, a club can no longer operate effectively. The work becomes too onerous for the few members, no matter how dedicated they may be.

Membership declines because people die, they move away, or they stop attending when the focus of their life changes. Sometimes a faction of a club breaks away because they feel their needs are not being met by the mother organization. Port Arthur Kansallisseura membership went through all of these upheavals.

In the financial journals of Kansallisseura, the entries for funeral flowers record the falling away of the dedicated old guard:

> Kalle Töyrä in 1949
> Kosti Koivukoski in 1952
> Jack Lankinen in 1955
> Veikko Rissanen in 1968
> Niilo Viitala in 1973
> Erkki Kuokkanen in 1978
> Liisa Lumiala in 1979
> Väinö Jacobson in 1981
> Ellen Poutanen in 1981
> Toini Jacobson in 1992
> Vieno Rita in 1995
> Klaus Tuisku in 1998

Farewell party for Reino Erkkilä in the summer of 1960. In the next two or three years all the members had left the Nor-Shor Club. Front row: Reino Erkkilä (joined the Canadian Navy), Raili Parviainen (went to university), Voitto Ylikorpi (got married). Back row: Anita Carlson (emigrated to Sweden), Olavi Laine (emigrated to Finland), Mårten Carlson (emigrated to Sweden), Håkan Carlson (emigrated to Sweden), Marjatta Lumiala (got married), Pekka Kuisma (emigrated to Finland), Raimo Mäntysalo (got married and moved to Toronto) and Kaarina Parviainen (got married and moved to Toronto) (From the collection of Marjatta Ylikorpi)

The Finnish Canadian Club, which operated in the late 1940s as a youth organization, separated from Kansallisseura around 1950. The young people wanted to run their activities in English, and felt more comfortable as an independent sports and charity club.

The Nor-Shor Club's demise, on the other hand, came about because its members scattered "to the four winds" in the early 1960s. School, marriage, travel, emigration and re-location took its toll on the once vibrant organization.

The same fate met the third set of youth clubbers in the late 1960s, and finally the Nor-Shor Club was declared defunct in 1971.

Kansallisseura records show that around 1985 membership levels fell by about 50% to a new plateau, which remained essentially the same until the end. These numbers were not enough to support major undertakings such as the Surprise Lake Swim. This had been the main activity of Kansallisseura for almost 30 years, but the club no longer had the necessary manpower to run it effectively after 1987.

Much of the club's fundraising for the next ten years was directed towards the upkeep of the Surprise Lake Camp. The flea markets, held in the late 1980s and early 1990s were especially successful, generating a total of almost $1,000.00 for this purpose. Midsummer dances continued until 1996, but often "there were more mosquitoes than people". Thus at the June 4, 1997 meeting it was decided that the number of people attending no longer justified hiring an orchestra, and so the long-running tradition ended.

For the last five years the upkeep of the Surprise Lake camp took most of the club's energies. At the May 31, 1999 meeting the executive decided unanimously that the camp would be sold the following year. In June, 2000 it was put up for sale with Heikki Väänänen Realty, and Erkki Sirén was assigned to find the boundary markers in the bush. The sale

Erkki Sirén performing his duties as "talonmies" (General Manager) at Surprise Lake camp (From the collection of Pentti Junni)

Entry on page 158 in the last Kansallisseura financial journal for January 21, 2003

was completed on August 13, 2001, and the last recorded meeting of *Port Arthurin Kansallisseura* (Finnish National Society) on April 11, 2002 dealt with the distribution of the funds.

However, the final entry for Port Arthur Kansallisseura, after the sale of the camp had been completed and all the books had been closed, is found on page 158 of the last financial journal.

"January 21, 2003

I am writing here a conclusion to Eko's work as a treasurer. Eko died suddenly at his home on the third of January, 2003, and this ended the long commitment of Erkki Kalevi Sirén in the service of Kansallisseura. Eko was the kind of responsible *"talonmies"* (general manager), who took care of the club's summer camp, and fixed whatever needed fixing. In him we lost a friend we will sorely miss and always remember. Signed: Pentti and others.

Eko's funeral service was held at Hilldale Lutheran Church on January 10, 2003."

Port Arthur Kansallisseura began in 1926 as the protector of "the White islands in the Red sea"[1]. Over the course of its life, it evolved in response to the push and pull of external circumstances, emerging in the mid 1950s as a non-political social club. This book has brought to life the members of this organization and has given the readers a glimpse into their activities. The people have been portrayed, not merely as names in recorded entries, but as dedicated, vibrant, funny, talented men and women, striving to make a difference in their time.

---

[1] Lindstrom-Best, Varpu, "Central Organization of the Loyal Finns in Canada," *Polyphony: The Bulletin of the Multicultural History Society of Ontario, Finns in Ontario*, (Vol. 3, No. 2, Fall 1981) p. 103.

120

Appendix I
Chronology

Some milestones in the 76 year history of Port Arthur Kansallisseura:

22.01.1926	Kansallisseura Turisti founding meeting held
24.01.1926	First executive meeting held
February, 1926	Sointu mixed choir joined Kansallisseura
28.02.1926	First Kalevala Day celebrated
10.03.1926	Official Opening Ceremony *(Alkajaisjuhla)* held
02.09.1926	Needlecraft Club *(Käsityökerho)* started
06.12.1926	First Independence Day celebrated
13.12.1926	First Christmas Party held at Wallace Hall
17.04.1928	Name changed to *Port Arthurin Kansallisseura* (Finnish National Society)
1929	Debating Club functioned during the year
1930	Two building lots purchased for $900.00, later sold
16.04.1930	4th Anniversary celebrated
24.04.1930	Sports & Gymnastic Club Kiri established
07.12.1930	Kansallisseura male choir sang for the first time
22.02.1931	Central Organization of Loyal Finns in Canada established in Toronto
March, 1931	First edition of *Kalevalainen Kansa* published
21.04.1931	5th Anniversary celebrated
18.04.1933	Joined COLFC as the Port Arthur branch
21.01.1934	Reading circle set up to raise money for library
25.11.1939	Finnish Aid Society established in Port Arthur
16.05.1941	Meeting to re-start Kansallissera held
18.03.1942	First social evening of re-started club held
04.05.1946	$500.00 collected over 4 years sent to Canada-Finland Aid Society Fund
09.01.1947	Finnish Canadian Club started
1950	Building lot on Algoma Street purchased, later sold
08.10.1951	Women's club re-activated
07.08.1952	Ball for Armi Kuusela, Miss Universe 1952, held
1954	Re-joined COLFC after leaving it in the mid 1930s
13.06.1954	Decision to purchase log cabin at Surprise Lake made
19.09.1954	First meeting at Surprise Lake camp held
24.01.1955	Purchase of Surprise Lake camp completed
June, 1955	Sauna at Surprise Lake camp built
19.05.1956	30th Anniversary Dance held
1957	Nor-Shor Club started
21.06.1958	First Midsummer Dance held at Surprise Lake camp
16.08.1959	First Surprise Lake Swim held
17.01.1960	Decision to tear down Surprise Lake log cabin made
May, 1960	Dance pavilion built at Surprise Lake
Summer, 1961	Separate saunas for men and women built
18.08.1964	Nor-Shor Club Dancers formed
23.10.1966	40th Anniversary Dance held
17.01.1971	Nor-Shor Club officially disbanded
02.10.1976	50th Anniversary Dance held
12.07.1987	Last Surprise lake Swim held
21.06.1996	Last Midsummer Dance held
31.05.1999	Decision to sell Surprise Lake camp taken
13.08.2001	Surprise Lake camp sold
11.04.2002	Last meeting of Port Arthur Kansallisseura recorded
2010	History of Port Arthur Kansallisseura published

Appendix II
Surprise Lake Swim Results

The results of the Surprise Lake Swim for the 29 years of its existence. No times are given, since the distances varied from year to year.

1959	
Men's Open (2.5 miles)	**Women's Open (0.75 miles)**
I Mårten Carlson	I Anita Carlson
II Teuvo Sorvisto	II Marjatta Lumiala
III Håkan Carlson	III Raili Parviainen
IV Mikko ?	IV Ines Parviainen

1960	
Men's Open (2.5 miles)	**Women's Open (2.5 miles)**
I Dieter Bommes	I Terttu Vuorinen
II Veikko Mikkonen	II Raili Parviainen
III Neil Graver	III Sirkka Wahlberg
IV Jack Gurney Sr	IV Liisa Lumiala
V Roland D'Aoust	V Anita Carlson
VI Raimo Mäntysalo	

1961	
Men's Open (2.5 miles)	**Women's Open (0.75 miles)**
I Dieter Bommes	I Terttu Vuorinen
II Jack Gurney Sr	II Sirkka Wahlberg
III Pekka Kuisma	III Ulla Jämsä
IV Kaj Wickström	IV Tuula Paananen
V Teuvo Sorvisto	
VI Unto Patvio	
VII Mauno Lehtomaa	

1962	
Men's Open (2.5 miles)	**Women's Open (0.75 miles)**
I Pat Hogan (11 yrs)	I Carol Franchi
II Allan McCormick	II Pam Powell
III Dieter Bommes	III Diana Humphreys
IV Jack Gurney Sr	IV Terttu Vuorinen
V Evan Newman	V Sharon Coghlan
VI Allan Saxberg (tie)	VI Sirkka Wahlberg
VI Teuvo Sorvisto (tie)	VII Ulla Jämsä
VIII Aarre Wahlberg	
IX John Milne	

1963

Men's Open (2.5 miles)
I   Al McCormick
II John Mair
III Jack Gurney Sr

High Diving Competition
I   Al McCormick
II Teuvo Sorvisto
III A. Arnamo

Women's Open (0.75 miles)
I   Pam Powell
II Jane McCormick
III Diana Humphreys

1964

Men's Open (2.5 miles)
I   Pat Hogan
II   Jim Donohue
III Allan Wildey
IV   Jack Gurney Sr
V   Peter Bodnar
VI   Don MacKay
VII Reino Sinervö
VIII Kaj Wickström
IX   Teuvo Sorvisto
X   Gilles Therrian

Women's Open (0.75 miles)
I   Cherie Tamblyn
II Jane McCormick
III Diana Humphreys
IV Terttu Vuorinen
V   Cindy Sabourin

1965

Men's Open (2.5 miles)
I   Pat Hogan

High Diving Competition
I   Jack Gurney Sr
II Lincoln Anderson
III Tapio Paalanen
IV Teuvo Sorvisto
V   Veikko Peltoniemi

Women's Open (0.75 miles)
I   Ruth Exley
II Jane McCormick
III Diana Humphreys

1966

Men's Open (2.5 miles)
- I Pat Hogan
- II John Exley (13 yrs)
- III Rod Harris (14 yrs)
- IV Frank Gelling
- V Peter Bodnar
- VI Jim Donohue
- VII Jack Gurney Sr
- VIII Len Gelling
- IX Kari Jämsä
- X Melvin Godick
- XI Martti Ahonen
- XII Reino Sinervö

Women's Open (0.75 miles)
- I Jane McCormick
- II Diana Humphreys
- III Lorna Pelto
- IV Liisa Räty

High Diving Competition
- I Peter Bodnar
- II Larry Eyers
- III Lincoln Anderson
- IV Reg Hogan
- V Glenn Charbon
- VI Osmo Bergroth (tie)
- VI Gordie Wilson (tie)
- VIII Henry Harja
- IX Kai Hilden
- X Gary Wilson

1967

Men's Open (2.5 miles)
- I Ari Rahkonen
- II Kaj Wickström

Children (10 years)
- I John Vesterinen
- II Marian Lähteenmäki

Children (12 years)
- I Scarlet Pöyhönen
- II Heidi Pöyhönen
- III Kari Vesterinen

1968

Men's Open (2.5 miles)
- I Raymond Ranta
- II Rodger Williams
- III Harry Curtis

Senior Men's Open (2.5 miles)
- I Jack Gurney Sr
- II Kaj Wickström
- III Unto Patvio

Women's Open (0.75 miles)
- I Diana Humphreys
- II Laurie Curtis
- III Susan Haavisto
- IV Anja Nenonen

1969

Men's Open (2.5 miles)
I   Rodger Williams
II Ray McDevitt
III Raymond Ranta
IV Kari Jämsä
V   Ahti Tabell

Senior Men's Open (2.5 miles)
I   Unto Patvio
II Kaj Wickström

Women's Open (0.75 miles)
I   Diana Humphreys
II Susan Collin
III Susan Haavisto
IV Mary McCormick
V   Eija Ranta (11 yrs)

1970

Men's Open (2.5 miles)
I   Rodger Williams
II Steve Menzies
III Ray McDevitt
IV John Arblaster

Senior Men's Open (2.5 miles)
I   Unto Patvio

Women's Open (0.75 miles)
I   Diana Humphreys
II Ann Hogan
III Susan Collin
IV Marian Lähteenmäki
V   Susan Haavisto

1971

Men's Open (2.5 miles)
I   Rodger Williams
II Jack Gurney Jr

Senior Men's Open (0.75 miles)
I   Jack Gurney Sr
II Kaj Wickström
III Toivo Laine
IV Unto Patvio

Women's Open (0.75 miles)
I   Kathy Donohue (11 yrs)
II Lisa Buset

1972

Men's Open (2.5 miles)
I   Pete Rutherford
II Rodger Williams
III Jay Safir
IV Jack Gurney Jr
V   John McKeown

Women's Open (0.75 miles)
I   Kathy Donohue
II Eija Ranta

Senior Men's Open (0.75 miles)
I   Jack Gurney Sr
II Kaj Wickström
III Pentti Wasenius
IV Unto Patvio
V   Taisto Miettinen

1973

Men's Open (2.5 miles)
- I   Jack Gurney Jr
- II John McKeown

Senior Men's Open (0.75 miles)
- I   Jack Gurney Sr
- II Kaj Wickström
- III Unto Patvio

Children under 12
- I   Ken Simi

Women's Open (0.75 miles)
- I   Michele Kreilmann
- II Kathy MacLeay
- III Eija Ranta
- IV Kaija Ranta

Children under 15
- I   Kari Silventoinen
- II Vesa Vanska
- III Tom Haavisto

1974

Men's Open (2.5 miles)
- I   Jari Lind (11 yrs)
- II Pete Rutherford
- III Mark Hlady

Senior Men's Open (0.75 miles)
- I   Jack Gurney Sr
- II Eepu Aksela
- III Tapio Paalanen
- IV Unto Patvio

Women's Open (0.75 miles)
- I   Kathy MacLeay
- II Jocelyn Wilkins
- III Carol Johnson
- IV Eija Ranta
- V   Kaija Ranta
- VI Heather Lauder

Children under 12
- I   Ken Simi

1975

Men's Open (2.5 miles)
- I   Mark Hlady
- II Jari Lind
- III Pete Rutherford
- IV Raymond Ranta

Senior Men's Open (0.75 miles)
- I   Unto Patvio

Women's Open (0.75 miles)
- I   Kathy MacLeay
- II Carol Johnson
- III Susan Johnson
- IV Tuija Jauho
- V   Irene Haavisto

1976

Men's Open (2.5 miles)
- I   Jim Donohue
- II Jari Lind
- III Mark Hlady
- IV Raymond Ranta

Senior Men's Open (0.75 miles)
- I   Unto Patvio

Women's Open (0.75 miles)
- I   Kathy MacLeay
- II Susan Johnson
- III Carol Johnson
- IV Wendy Nojonen
- V   Kaija Ranta

1977	
Men's Open (2.5 miles)	**Women's Open (0.75 miles)**
I Jack Donohue	I Kathy MacLeay
II Brian Pellizzari	II Wendy Nojonen
	III Kathy Ahola
	IV Kathy Donohue

1978	
Men's Open (2.5 miles)	**Women's Open (0.75 miles)**
I Jack Donohue	I Wendy Nojonen
II Jukka Wäissi	
III Bill Boswell	**Senior Men's Open (0.75 miles)**
	I Eino Ranta
	II Unto Patvio
	III Nils Inkilä

1979	
Men's Open (2.5 miles)	**Women's Open (0.75 miles)**
I Jim Donohue	I Wendy Nojonen
II Jari Lind	II Liisa Hämäläinen
III Jukka Wäissi	III Leena Hämäläinen
	IV Seija Hämäläinen
Senior Men's Open (0.75 miles)	V Sherry Huotari
I Pete Rutherford	VI Kaija Ranta
II Eepu Aksela	
III Mel Kempe	
IV Unto Patvio	

1980	
Men's Open (2.5 miles)	**Women's Open (0.75 miles)**
I Jari Lind	I Wendy Nojonen
II John Ranta	
III Mike Wright	**Senior Men's Open (0.75 miles)**
IV Kim Hutch	I Pete Rutherford
V Jari Leinonen	II Eino Ranta
	III Unto Patvio
	IV Taisto Miettinen

1981

Men's Open (2.5 miles)
I	Jim Donohue
II	Jari Lind
III	Bill Boswell
IV	John Ranta
V	Hugh Brown
VI	Tony Hatherly
VII	Jari Leinonen
VIII	Alfred Tomasini

Women's Open (0.75 miles)
I	Wendy Nojonen
II	Lori Byerley
III	Sherry Huotari
IV	Carlies Giles
V	Marian Lähteenmäki
VI	Kaija Ranta

Senior Men's Open (0.75 miles)
I	Pete Rutherford
II	Eepu Aksela
III	Unto Patvio

1982

Men's Open (0.75 miles)
I	Bill Boswell
II	Kim Hutch
III	Hugh Brown

Women's Open (0.75 miles)
I	Pam Brown
II	Heli Ketola

Senior Men's Open (0.75 miles)
I	Mikko Kittilä
II	Unto Patvio
III	Taisto Miettinen

1983

Men's Open (1500 m)
I	Kevin O'Brian
II	Bill Boswell
III	John Corcoran
IV	Brian Berry
V	Larry Moro

Women's Open (1000 m)
I	Eileen Puurala
II	Marilyn Milenko
III	Kathaleen Tulin

Senior Men's Open (1000 m)
I	Pete Rutherford
II	Mikko Kittilä
III	Hugh Brown
IV	Eino Ranta
V	Unto Patvio

1984

Men's Open (1500 m)
- I   Bill Boswell
- II Peter Crooks
- III John Corcoran
- IV John Ranta
- V   Tony McQuilter
- VI Mike Wright
- VII Roberto Demero

Senior Men's Open (1200 m)
- I   Sandy Stalker
- II Pete Rutherford
- III Eino Ranta
- IV Unto Patvio

Women's Open (1200 m)
- I   Anne Bodak
- II J. Sillman-Stalker
- III Carrie Charban (11 yrs)
- IV Norine Oda
- V   Pam Dawes
- VI Eileen Puurula
- VII Gail Tulin

1985

Men's Open (1500 m)
- I   Paul White
- II Bill Boswell
- III Ken Björn
- IV John Ranta
- V   John Corcoran

Senior Men's Open (1200 m)
- I   Lorne McDougal
- II Jim Miller
- III Peter Rutherford
- IV Bruce Corness
- V   Brian Berry
- VI Unto Patvio

Women's Open (1200 m)
- I   Lorraine Dilca
- II Carrie Charban
- III Patti Palinka
- IV Wendy Rissanen (11 yr)
- V   Cherry Huotari
- VI Norma Fillpovic

1986

Men's Open (1600 m)
- I   Ken Paradis
- II   Glen Halvorson (11 yrs)
- III Todd Stock
- IV   Ken Björn
- V   Robert Kavanagh
- VI   Bill Boswell
- VII Grant Mitchell
- VIII Victor Ritchie
- IX   Kevin Kennedy
- X   Kim Hutch
- XI   Doug Niemi
- XII Jari Leinonen

Women's Open (1200 m)
- I   Wendy Rissanen
- II Lorraine Dilca
- III Carrie Charban
- IV Joanne Boulter (11 yrs)
- V   Debbie Ritchie
- VI Caryn Charban (10 yrs)

Senior Men's Open (1200 m)
- I   Peter Rutherford

1987	
Men's Open (1500 m) I Bill Boswell II John Corcoran III Kevin Rissanen IV Vello Merelaid	**Women's Open (1200 m)** I Wendy Rissanen II Marian Begall III Sandra Sutherland **Senior Men's Open (1200 m)** I Peter Rutherford II Gordon Arges

Appendix III
Kansallisseura Members

Year = Year member's name first appeared in Port Arthur Kansallisseura records
Comments
  Auditor = Auditor of Founding Executive
  Award = Membership awarded for working at Surprise Lake Camp
  BK = Bookkeeper of Founding Executive
  CM = Chairman of Founding Executive
  DM = Deputy Member of Founding Executive
  FC Club = Finnish Canadian Club member
  FM = Founding Member
  GM = General Manager of Founding Executive
  HC = Honorary Chairman with year of award
  HM = Honorary Member with year of award
  MS = Membership Secretary of Founding Executive
  Secretary = Secretary of Founding Executive
  Treasurer = Treasurer of Founding Executive
  VC = Vice-Chairman of Founding Executive

Name of Member	Year	Comments
Aarnio, Anna	1928	
Adams, W.	1950	FC Club
Adams, Mrs. W.	1950	FC Club
Ahlstrand, Doris	1959	
Aho, Ida	1953	
Aho, Marie	1964	
Aho, Tyyne	1932	
Ahokas, Hannu	1964	
Ahokas, Hellin	1963	
Ahokas, Olavi	1962	
Ahokas, Vieno	1965	
Ahokas, Vilho	1965	
Ahola, Maire	1964	
Albrecht, Esteri	1946	
Alkquist, Leila	1967	
Annala, E.	1929	
Annala, Heikki	1951	
Annala, Martta	1929	
Arnam, Marja-Leena	1964	
Arvo, Pauli	1965	
Aunala, Einari	1930	
Autio, Elsa	1926	FM
Autio, Kalle	1930	
Beck, Anna	1932	
Beck, Gustav Alfred	1930	
Björn, Martti	1960	
Carlson, Anita	1958	
Carlson, Gerda	1959	
Carlson, Håkan	1958	
Carlson, Henry	1959	
Carlson, Mårten	1958	
Davidson, Anna	1926	

Name of Member	Year	Comments
Elo, Aarne	1955	
Elonen, Arto	1970	
Elonen, Taina	1978	
Elonen, Virva	1983	
Erkkilä, Anna	1958	
Erkkilä, Henry	1979	
Erkkilä, Pia	1979	
Erkkilä, Reino	1958	
Erkkilä, Sirkka	1968	
Erkkilä, Toivo	1958	
Euren, Kalle	1932	
Fentti, W.	1933	
Finell	1926	
Forsberg, Mrs.	1952	
Frilander, Aksel	1930	
Galisalo, Niilo	1958	
Gohlin, Mrs. A.	1952	
Greta, Anja	1972	
Haapaaho, Antti	1965	
Haapsaari, Pentti	1971	
Haapsaari, Petri	1970	
Haapsaari, Ritva	1980	
Haavisto, Anja	1973	
Haavisto, Eero	1930	
Haavisto, Kaarina	1967	
Haavisto, Mikko	1968	
Haavisto, Olavi	1967	
Hagert, Vilho	1948	
Hahka, Erkki	1932	
Hahka, Matti	1932	
Haikonen, Liisa	1966	
Haikonen, Pauli	1965	

Name of Member	Year	Comments
Haikonen, Pentti	1966	
Haikonen, Raili	1966	
Haikonen, Tuija	1965	
Halonen, W.	1950	FC Club
Hämäläinen, Mrs. Ville	1952	
Hämäläinen, Ville	1960	
Hammarberg, Amanda	1926	
Hammarberg	1926	
Hankila, Anja	1971	
Hankila, Juhani	1971	
Hankila, Mikko	1969	
Hankilanoja, Anja	1970	
Hannula, Richard	1930	
Harju, Mrs.	1952	
Hartikainen, Sinikka	1959	
Haukila, Anja	1972	
Hautala, Helena	1960	
Hautala, Sulo	1960	
Häyrynen, Erick	1928	
Hed	1926	
Heikkilä, L.	1932	
Heikurinen, A.	1958	
Heinonen	1981	
Heiskanen, Otto	1932	
Heiskanen, Paavo	1933	
Helenius, Antero	1970	
Helenius, Vuokko	1970	
Helin, A.	1974	
Helin, H.	1980	
Hendrickson, Eeli	1926	FM
Hendrickson, Lilli	1926	FM
Hietala	1954	Award
Hietanen, Anni	1948	
Hietaranta, Paavo	1927	
Hiltunen, Mrs.	1944	
Hintikka, Hjalmar	1948	
Hintikka, J.	1950	
Hirvasoja, Anja	1959	
Hirvasoja, Risto	1959	
Hirvonen, Emil	1932	
Hirvonen, Kerttu	1959	
Hirvonen, Pentti	1957	
Hoffren, Pirjo	1959	
Hoffren, Topi	1961	
Hokkanen, L.	1932	
Hollanti	1966	
Holm, Mrs. W.	1926	
Holm, W.	1926	
Holman, Marlene	1958	
Honkaniemi, Martta	1929	
Hulkko, Olavi	1959	
Hynnä, Kaarlo	1962	
Hynnä, Pirkko	1964	
Hyvönen, Vilho	1928	

Name of Member	Year	Comments
Isosaari, Ann-Gret	1971	
Isotalo, Meri	1950	
Isotalo, Toivo	1950	
Itkonen, Annikki	1967	
Itkonen, Taisto	1967	
Jaakkola, Aili	1963	
Jaakkola, Hilda	1948	
Jacobson, Toini	1947	HM/64
Jacobson, Väinö	1947	HM/64
Jacobson, Väinö Jr.	1961	
Jacobson, Vera	1926	FM, HM/56
Jacobson, Walter	1926	FM
Jämsä, Marjaana	1968	
Jämsä, Ulla	1959	
Jansson, Lars	1959	
Jantunen, J.	1932	
Järvi, Hilja	1932	
Järvinen, Milja	1932	
Järvinen, Toivo	1932	
Jauhiainen, Matti	1928	
Jauhiainen, Taneli	1928	
Jokela, Matti	1962	
Jokelainen, Aino	1963	
Jokelainen, Paul	1963	
Jousmäki, Johanna	1971	
Jousmäki, Toivo	1970	
Jukola, A.	1954	Award
Junni, Pentti	1960	
Junni, Reetta	1960	
Justin, K.	1926	
Justin, Mrs. K.	1926	
Kaari, Olavi	1967	
Kallio, Armas	1929	
Kallio, D.	1932	
Kallio, L.	1933	
Kallio, Sanni	1926	FM
Kallio, W.	1954	Award
Kangas, Yrjö	1930	
Kankaansydän, A.	1926	
Kareno, Niilo	1966	
Kärkkäinen, Alpo	1958	
Kärkkäinen, Liisa	1966	
Kärkkäinen, Vilho	1926	
Kärkkänen, K.	1961	
Karonen, Armas	1930	
Karppainen	1951	
Karttunen, Arne	1927	
Karttunen, Kalle	1931	
Karttunen, Maire	1965	
Karttunen, Tyyne	1948	HM/64
Kasala, K.	1963	
Kasari, Laimi	1932	
Kassela, A.	1951	
Kassela, M.	1951	

Name of Member	Year	Comments
Kastarinen, Olli	1928	
Kauhanen, Eemeli	1930	
Kemppainen, Kalervo	1969	
Ketola, Hanna	1975	
Ketola, Kauno	1972	
Ketola, P.	1930	
Ketonen, L.	1950	FC Club
Ketonen, P.	1978	
Ketonen, Tauno	1949	FC Club
Ketonen, William	1931	
Kettunen, Pekka	1947	
Kilponen, Kirsti	1950	
Kittilä, Kaisu	1983	
Kittilä, Mikko	1983	
Kivilahti, Edla	1932	
Kivilahti, Matti	1926	
Köhlin, Annikki	1963	
Köhlin, August	1951	
Koiranen, Ellen	1964	
Koiranen, Niilo	1962	
Koivukoski, Edit	1926	FM
Koivukoski, Kai	1949	FC Club
Koivukoski, Kosti	1926	FM, CM, HC/31
Koivuniemi, Yrjö	1948	
Kojola, Aina	1959	
Kojola, Marie	1959	
Kokko, Mrs.	1952	
Kokko, Väinö	1930	
Kokkonen, Hanna	1928	
Kokkonen, Sinikka	1984	
Koklin, A.	1951	
Kolehmainen, Kaisa	1968	
Kolehmainen, Kyösti	1960	
Kolehmainen, Matti	1967	
Kolkka, S.	1951	
Konu, Kalervo	1975	
Konu, Sirkka	1975	
Korhonen, Väinö	1930	
Korolainen, Hanna	1930	
Korolainen, Lauri	1928	
Korolainen, Rauha	1930	
Korpela, Alpo Taisto	1959	
Korpela, Anna Maija	1959	
Korpela, Eliisa	1959	
Korpi, Aila	1959	
Korpi, Anja	1959	
Korpi, Jaakko	1968	
Korte, Erick J.	1926	FM, GM
Korte, Hilja	1926	FM, Secretary
Korte, Jack	1929	
Koski, Meeri	1959	
Kosola, Kusti	1964	
Kotanen, Hjalmar	1948	
Kotanen, Mary	1948	

Name of Member	Year	Comments
Kotanen, Niilo	1948	
Kovalainen, Lauri	1931	
Kowalski, Margery	1965	
Kraft, Paavo	1974	
Kraft, Pirkko	1970	
Kruus, E.	1982	
Kuisma, Aini	1964	
Kuisma, Armas	1964	
Kuisma, Pekka	1958	
Kumpulainen, Arvi	1930	
Kuokkanen, Erkki	1951	
Kuokkanen, Jussi	1978	
Kuokkanen, Pirjo	1978	
Kuokkanen, Ruth	1952	
Kyrö, Niilo	1926	FM, BK
Kyrö, Mrs. Niilo	1934	
Kyyhkynen, Anni	1930	
Kyyhkynen, Pirkko	1930	
Laaja, Kalle	1929	
Laakko, Liisa	1968	
Laakso, Armas	1930	
Laakso, Sirkka-Liisa	1959	
Laaksonen, K.	1958	
Laamanen, T.	1960	
Lahdenperä, H.	1950	
Lahdenperä, Heikki	1948	
Lahdenperä, Mrs.	1946	
Lähteenmäki, Marjatta	1967	
Lahti, Aili	1946	
Lahti, Siinto	1947	
Laine, Olavi	1958	
Laine, P.	1952	
Laitinen, Elli	1957	
Laitinen, Matti	1957	
Laitinen, Paavo	1930	
Laitinen, Paula	1959	
Lampo, Arja	1964	
Lampo, Pirjo	1964	
Lamppu, A.	1979	
Lamppu, B.	1979	
Langen, A.	1950	FC Club
Langen, R.	1950	FC Club
Langren, M.	1950	FC Club
Lankinen, Heikki	1951	
Lankinen, Hilja	1948	
Lankinen, Jack	1931	
Lankinen, P.	1951	
Lankinen, Rauni	1951	
Lappalainen	1954	Award
Laskujärvi, Urpo	1959	
Lassi, Aleksi	1926	
Lassi, Helmi	1926	
Lastajärvi, U.	1982	
Latvala, Viola	1930	

Name of Member	Year	Comments
Latvio, Vappu	1959	
Lehtinen, Eino	1961	
Lehtinen, Saimi	1968	
Leino, Hilma	1948	
Leinonen, Maiju	1926	FM, MS
Leppänen, S.	1950	FC Club
Leskelä, Taina	1973	
Lind, Marja Leena	1971	
Lind, Raimo	1965	
Linden, D.	1961	
Linden, G.	1958	
Linden, Helen	1958	
Linden, John	1955	
Lindqvist, Mrs.	1926	
Louhenlahti, I.	1951	
Loukila, Yrjö	1929	
Lumiala, Liisa	1958	
Lumiala, Marjatta	1958	
Lumiala, Pauli	1958	
Luoma, Mauno	1980	
Luomala, Aarne	1964	
Luomala, Helena	1958	
Lusenius, V.	1932	
Mahlamäki, Veikko	1932	
Mahlamäki, Vieno	1932	
Maijala, L.	1980	
Maijala, Rauha	1983	
Maja, Yrjö	1954	Award
Majanen, Kalle	1930	
Majanmaa, Sirkka	1967	
Mäkäräinen, Erkki	1962	
Mäkelä, Eeva	1969	
Mäkelä, Eino	1969	
Mäkelä, Laila	1957	
Mäkelä, Pentti	1958	
Mäkelä, Väinö	1957	
Mäki, Andrea	1970	
Mäki, Anni	1929	
Mäki, Eeli	1962	
Mäki, Elsie	1969	
Mäki, Hermanni	1967	
Mäki, John	1926	
Mäki, Kaarlo	1948	
Mäki, Kaija	1993	
Mäki, Leonard W.	1926	FM, VC
Mäki, O.	1963	
Mäki, Tyyne	1926	FM
Mäki, Väinö	1932	
Mäki, Veijo	1968	
Mäki, Viljo	1929	
Mäkinen, Eeva	1969	
Mäkinen, Meeri	1969	
Mäkinen, Olli	1964	
Mäkiniemi, Eino	1931	

Name of Member	Year	Comments
Mäkitalo, Sten	1932	
Mannila, Hilja	1950	
Mannila, Maino	1962	
Mannila, Sulo	1950	
Mäntysalo, Raimo	1959	
Marjakangas, Kerttu	1932	
Marjanen, Virva	1983	
Martikainen, Eero	1969	
Martikainen, Marjaana	1970	
Martin, Mary	1944	
Mattila, Vilho	1932	
Maunu, Fred	1932	
Maunu, Lauri	1926	FM, Treasurer
Metsä, Arttu	1960	
Mickelson, Andrew	1927	
Miettinen, Helmi	1971	
Miettinen, Pekka	1970	
Miettinen, Taisto	1976	
Miettinen, Terho	1971	
Mikkola, Jalo	1932	
Molin, Mrs.	1944	
Mononen, Mauno	1927	
Murtokorpi, Ilmari	1962	
Murtokorpi, Iris	1962	
Mustonen, Helli	1965	
Mustonen, Mikko	1954	Award
Mustonen, Mrs.	1928	
Mustonen, Siiri	1962	
Mutka, Teuvo	1964	
Mutka, Tuula	1964	
Myllymaa, Aapo	1967	
Myllymaa, Katriina	1984	
Myllymaa, Sinikka	1967	
Myyryläinen, L.	1963	
Myyryläinen, M.	1963	
Näsi, Väinö	1926	
Nelson, Hilda	1947	
Nelson, Ingrid	1930	
Nelson, Yrjö	1932	
Nenonen, Anja	1969	
Niemelä, John	1953	
Niemelä, Sylvia	1953	
Niemi, P.	1954	Award
Niemi, Reino	1932	
Niemi, Toivo	1930	
Niemistö, Lyyli	1930	
Nihtilä, Paavo	1948	
Niinimäki, H.W.	1926	FM, Auditor
Nikander, K.	1926	
Nikander, Mrs.	1926	
Niku, Saima	1926	
Niskala, Eeli	1930	
Niskala, Paavo	1954	Award
Niskanen, Eli	1955	

Name of Member	Year	Comments
Nummelin, Maire	1971	
Nummelin, Matti	1971	
Nurmela, Aukusti	1967	
Nurmi, Vihtori	1928	
Nuutinen, Raili	1958	
Nykänen, Raimo	1966	
Nyström, Hillevi	1969	
Ohraniemi, E.	1932	
Oikonen, Mrs. William	1934	
Oja, Nick	1964	
Ojala, August	1947	
Ojaniemi, Reino	1959	
Ojanperä, A.	1981	
Ojanperä, K.	1981	
Oksanen, A.	1951	
Oksman, Alpo	1951	
Ollikainen, Eino	1968	
Ollikainen, K.	1932	
Ollikkala, Joe	1931	
Orrenmaa, K.	1930	
Oxman, Jasenk	1952	
Paananen, M.	1927	
Paananen, Maria	1932	
Paananen, Vieno	1926	FM, DM
Paavola, Glenn	1964	
Pahikainen, Alpo	1959	
Pahikainen, Hanna	1959	
Paju, Emil	1929	
Pakka, Hanna	1946	
Pakka, Uuno	1932	
Pakka, W.	1949	
Palkeinen, Yrjö	1927	
Palokangas, Ville	1984	
Pantti	1960	
Pantti, Mrs.	1960	
Pärssinen, Alma	1952	
Pärssinen, Arvo	1954	Award
Partanen, Rainer	1968	
Parviainen, Lea	1959	
Parviainen, Ines	1959	
Parviainen, Kaarina	1958	
Parviainen, Raili	1958	
Parviainen, Toini	1952	
Parviainen, Veijo	1959	
Parviainen, Veikko	1959	
Paukkunen, Elsa	1954	
Paukkunen, Ivari	1955	
Paulanen, E.	1953	
Pehkonen, Hilkka	1973	
Pehkonen, Niilo	1972	
Pehkonen, Sirkka	1972	
Pekkala, M.	1932	
Pelkonen, Helmi	1926	
Pelto	1964	

Name of Member	Year	Comments
Pelto, Mrs.	1964	
Peltola, Frank	1964	
Peltola, Lasse	1958	
Peltola, Mrs.	1950	
Peltola, Signe	1963	
Peltola, T.	1950	
Peltonen, Aino	1965	
Peltonen, Aki	1968	
Peltonen, Urho	1965	
Pentti, Antero	1957	
Pentti, Salli	1969	
Pentti, Väinö	1926	FM, DM
Perä, Eero	1930	
Pesonen, Esko	1968	
Petäjä	1926	
Peterson, Eric	1949	FC Club
Pietarinen, Toivo	1952	
Pihlaja, Tarmo	1970	
Pihlojaniemi, Aimo	1930	
Piirto, Arvo	1932	
Piirto, Yrjö	1948	
Pilbacka, Paparin	1970	
Pinala, Pekka	1959	
Pitkänen, Martti	1929	
Pitkänen, Ritva	1984	
Pleson, K.	1950	FC Club
Pleson, S.	1950	FC Club
Pohjoispää, H.	1982	
Poutanen, Ellen	1927	HM/64
Poutanen, Rafael	1928	
Poutanen, Ralph	1926	HM/64
Pöysti, A.	1932	
Pulkkinen, Ester	1932	
Pulkkinen, K.	1963	
Puumala	1926	
Puuska, Suoma	1926	
Puuska, Toivo	1926	
Puustinen, Matti	1927	
Rannankari, Marita	1963	
Rannankari, Untamo	1963	
Ranta, Ellen	1962	
Ranta, Harold	1962	
Rantala, Jaakko	1928	
Ranta-ojala, Reijo	1964	
Rathje, Brian	1968	
Räty, Marja Liisa	1967	
Räty, Pertti	1965	
Räty, Rauno	1965	
Rautio, L.	1979	
Rautio, M.	1979	
Räystölä, Frank	1930	
Richmond, Mrs.	1952	
Riekkö, Arvo	1977	
Riippi	1954	Award

Name of Member	Year	Comments
Rintaniemi, T.	1930	
Rissanen, Richard	1954	
Rissanen, Saimi	1953	HM/64
Rissanen, Veikko	1953	HM/64
Ristimäki, Arvi	1929	
Rita, Aarne	1926	HM/64
Rita, Vieno	1926	FM, HM/64
Romu, Lauri	1952	
Romu, Leila	1952	
Ronala, P.	1954	Award
Rönkkö, Juho	1928	
Rönkkö, Kerttu	1944	
Rönkkö, Mikko	1930	
Ruotsalainen, J.F.	1926	
Ruuska, Silja	1948	
Ryti, Alfred	1929	
Saari, J.	1932	
Saari, Risto	1967	
Saarinen, Fiilus	1930	
Saastamoinen, Armas	1933	
Saastamoinen, H.	1932	
Saasto, Hannes	1962	
Säisä, Juho	1928	
Salmela, Eino	1930	
Salmela, Vilho	1969	
Salmi, Erkki	1957	
Salmi, Terttu	1957	
Salmijärvi, A.	1963	
Salmijärvi, E.	1963	
Salonen, Martta	1946	
Salonen, Martti	1950	
Salonen, Tuure	1948	
Särkijärvi, E.	1978	
Särkijärvi, J.	1978	
Särkkä, Erika	1981	
Särkkä, Jari	1980	
Särkkä, Maija	1982	
Särkkä, Sinikka	1980	
Särkkä, Väinö	1980	
Saukkonen, Uuno	1929	
Savo, Anni	1933	
Savolainen, Anni	1928	
Savolainen, Fileman	1929	
Savolainen, Kaarlo	1927	
Saxberg, Alfred	1926	FM
Saxberg, Mrs. A.	1926	FM
Saxberg, Yrjö	1926	FM
Schrey, R.	1926	FM, Auditor
Seppälä, Aune	1946	
Siddal, J.	1950	FC Club
Sihvonen, Anni	1968	
Sillanpää, Pauli	1950	
Sillanpää, Viola	1950	
Silventoinen, Liisa	1971	
Silventoinen, Seppo	1971	
Similä, W.	1950	
Simpson, Erika	1983	
Simpson, Ken	1983	
Sipilä, Helga	1969	
Sipilä, Herman	1969	
Sirén, Erkki	1959	
Smolander, Aune	1952	
Smolander, Onni	1960	
Sora, Eeva	1962	
Sora, Viljo	1962	
Sorri, Pirkko	1986	
Sorri, Simo	1986	
Sorvisto, Kirsti	1961	
Sorvisto, Teuvo	1958	
Stalhammar, Anna	1927	
Stalhammar, Kerttu	1927	
Stenback, Hilda	1944	
Stenback, Sophia	1929	
Still, Yrjö	1958	
Suikkari, Martti	1965	
Suline, Irene	1926	FM, HM/56
Suline, John E.	1929	
Sundell, Jenny	1954	
Sunila, Bruno	1963	
Sunila, Pirjo	1963	
Suuronen, Emil	1926	
Suutari, John	1954	Award
Suvanto, Eeva-Liisa	1964	
Suvanto, Katarina	1963	
Suvanto, Oskar	1963	
Syri, Ensiö	1962	
Syri, Kyllikki	1962	
Syrjä, Kalle	1978	
Taimela, Hilkka	1971	
Taimela, Matti	1971	
Tammela, Eeli	1929	
Tapio, Verneri	1927	
Tenant, Mrs.	1952	
Tenhunen, Matti	1930	
Tenkula, Urho	1926	
Tennant, Mrs.	1952	
Tiihonen, Aino	1962	
Tiihonen, Väinö	1962	
Tiitto, Aate	1928	
Tiitto, Aila	1959	
Tikkanen, Ester	1930	
Tikkanen, Olli	1926	FM
Tikkanen, Paavo	1947	
Tiura, K.	1926	
Tolvanen, Helmi	1950	
Tolvanen, Kaarlo	1950	
Tonts, Julius	1974	
Tonts, Vieno	1973	

Name of Member	Year	Comments
Toukkola, W.	1950	FC Club
Töyrä, Aune	1929	
Töyrä, Carl (Kalle)	1932	HM/33
Tuisku, Aimo	1953	
Tuisku, Klaus	1959	
Tuisku, Linnea	1944	
Tuisku, Pirkko	1959	
Tulin, Lena	1965	
Tuomela, Vieno	1952	
Tuomi, Arvo	1947	
Tuomi, Matilda	1926	FM, HM/64
Tuomialho, Lasse	1964	
Tuominen, Hilma	1948	
Tuomisto, Heimar	1968	
Turunen, Mikko	1930	
Unkuri, Lilja	1930	
Uurainen, Aila	1959	
Uusitalo, Hilja	1977	
Uusitalo, Kalevi	1977	
Vähäaho, Topi	1959	
Vahonen, Elli	1972	
Vahonen, Niilo	1972	
Vainikka, Lahja	1944	
Vainikka, Valde	1947	
Väisänen	1926	
Vala, Yrjö	1930	
Välilä, Eino	1978	
Valkama, Hilja	1959	
Valkama, Antti	1959	
Välkkilä, Lauri	1958	
Valmari, Antti	1928	
Vanhapelto, Hanna	1975	
Vanhapelto, Martti	1972	
Vänskä, Kauko	1952	
Vänskä, Raili	1969	
Vartiainen, Elsa	1964	
Vartiainen, Veikko	1964	
Vastamäki, Aino	1962	
Vastamäki, Hilkka	1963	
Vataja, Martti	1958	
Vataja, Sinikka	1968	
Vataja, Toini	1958	
Vertanen, Martha	1926	FM
Vesa, Uuno	1957	
Veste, Olavi	1970	
Vesterinen, Anna Liisa	1962	
Vesterinen, Liisa	1969	
Vesterinen, Olavi	1961	
Vickström, Helena	1962	
Vickström, Kaj	1962	
Vihtari, Annikki	1959	
Vihtari, Eljas	1959	
Viitala, Jackie	1950	
Viitala, Kirsti	1947	HM/64

Name of Member	Year	Comments
Viitala, Niilo	1947	HM/64
Viljakainen, Elis	1959	
Viljakainen, Helli	1952	
Viola, Hannes	1927	
Viola, Hilda	1927	
Virkkunen, Kalle	1933	
Virta, Anne	1978	
Virta, Elma	1978	
Virtanen, Ida	1926	FM, HM/33
Virtanen, Kalle	1926	FM, DM
Vuorijärvi, Martti	1928	
Vuorimaa, Joel	1929	
Wainikka, Lahja	1946	
Wickman, E.	1930	
Ylänen, Yrjö	1960	
Ylijoki, H.	1963	
Ylijoki, P.	1963	
Ylikorpi, Voitto	1958	
Ylikoski, Eero	1930	
Ylituomi, Arvo	1929	
Ylituomi, Tilda	1929	
Ylönen, Aulis	1964	

Appendix IV
References

Harpelle, Ronald & Lindstrom, Varpu & Pogorelskin, Alexis, editors, *Karelian Exodus – Finnish Communities in North America and Soviet Karelia during the Depression Era,* (Toronto: special issue of the *Journal of Finnish Studies*, Vol. 8, No. 1, August, 2004)

Ikola, J.O., V*aasan Jaakkoo rapakon takana 1947 – 48,* (Helsinki: Werner Söderström Osakeyhtiö, 1949)

Junni, Pentti, *Siirtolaisen Muistomerkki: The Immigrants Monument,* (Thunder Bay: 1976)

Lindstrom, Varpu, *From Heroes to Enemies, Finns in Canada, 1937 – 1947,* (Beaverton: Aspasia Books, 2000)

Raivio, Yriö, *Kanadan Suomalaisten Historia,* (Vancouver: New West Press Co. Ltd., 1975)

Toiviainen, Lauri, *75-vuotias Vapaa Sana, Lukijainsa omistama sanomalehti,* (Toronto: Vapaa Sana Press Ltd., 2008)

Tolvanen, Ahti, *Finntown, A Perspective on Urban Integration, Port Arthur Finns in the Inter-war Period: 1918 – 1939,* (University of Helsinki, Finn Forum, 1984)

—, *Canadan Uutiset,* (Port Arthur: back copies on microfilm from 1927 to 1951)

—, *Polyphony: The Bulletin of the Multicultural History Society of Ontario, Finns in Ontario, Vol. 3, No. 2,* (Toronto: Fall 1981)

—, *Vancouver Finlandia Club: Uudet juuret—Uudet tuulet,* (Vancouver: New West Press Co. Ltd., 2006)

Minutes of Meetings, Port Arthur Kansallisseura:

    January 22, 1926 to April 26, 1932
    November 29, 1949 to November 15, 1953
    October 8, 1951 to October 3, 1952
    March 21, 1954 to March 20, 1955
    February 4, 1960 to November 19, 1964
    January 12, 1964 to August 8, 1982
    February 8, 1983 to April 11, 2002

Financial Journals, Port Arthur Kansallisseura:

    March 18, 1942 to December 6, 1947
    March 18, 1942 to February 12, 1954
    February 29, 1944 to November 29, 1949
    January 7, 1947 to December 7, 1947
    January 7, 1947 to February 7, 1948
    March 15, 1954 to October, 1968
    March 4, 1958 to December 31, 1960
    January 1, 1963 to September 2, 1969
    January 30, 1967 to January 9, 1977
    December 1, 1976 to October 3, 2002

www.ingramcontent.com/pod-product-compliance
Lightning Source LLC
Chambersburg PA
CBHW081457040426
42446CB00016B/3283